CHRISTIAN
TO THE CORE

INTERNATIONAL LEADERSHIP INSTITUTE

V2

INTERNATIONAL LEADERSHIP INSTITUTE

ISBN 978-194328089-6

The cover is designed by award-winning graphic designer, Jeff Gribble.

Welcome to the Core

Life for an **oak tree** begins as an acorn.

But with time and the right conditions...

the acorn becomes a *majestic oak tree.*

A God-shaped life is illustrated in the Bible as a flourishing tree planted by God through the work of his hands. Those who trust in God and make him their confidence can be like a tree planted by a stream of water, whose leaves are always green and always bears fruit. When Jesus announced his ministry to a brokenhearted and enslaved world by reading from the scroll of Isaiah, he said he would not just heal people but that he could transform them into "oaks of righteousness." [1]

When you become a follower of Christ, the seed of discipleship is planted in your life. God's desire is that you develop deep roots, grow strong, and experience his full power and presence. Unfortunately, too many disciples never fully develop and suffer the consequences of a shallow life. In a recent six-year study by Christian researcher and author, George Barna, ten stages are identified in the Christian journey for fully experiencing God and his wholeness. According to Barna, only one in twenty Christians (5%), move past stage six. God desires that every disciple experience all ten stages. [2]

Christian to the Core is your twelve-session journey to becoming a deeper disciple by increasing your intimacy with God, increasing your love for people, and discovering God's greater purposes for your life. Get ready to explore the Eight Core Values of the most vibrant and dynamic Christians on planet earth, discovered through global research by the International Leadership Institute. You can use it alone, but this exciting resource is best used in a small group where you can study, share, and pray with others.

Just as a tree grows from the core, you also have the ability to grow when you focus on the core of who you are and what you can become in Christ. This journey can transform your life, relationships, and legacy.

Until all worship,

Wes and Joy Griffin
International Directors

Instructions for the Discussion Guide

Christian to the Core is based on the globally recognised leadership and discipleship curriculum used in more than 80 nations by the International Leadership Institute. This Discussion Guide provides an additional page at the end of each session to assist you in group discussions along this journey. For more resources, visit ChristiantotheCore.org or Facebook.com/ChristiantotheCore.

Register Today

Register yourself as a leader or group member at ChristiantotheCore.org/Register. You will receive specific updates to encourage you on the *Christian to the Core* journey.

Using the Curriculum

Most small groups meet twelve times with each session lasting one hour. Some small groups spend two weeks in each session to allow more time for in depth discussions. Depending on your context, you may choose to include fellowship, worship, and refreshments. It is important to cover the entire resource; each Core Value is essential.

For the maximum benefit, complete each session in your notebook before coming to that particular session. *Christian to the Core* relies heavily on group discussion and interaction. At some discussion points, a larger group can be broken into smaller groups for more interaction. Good discussions increase learning and personal transformation. A general outline for each session includes:

1. **Opening Prayer** – Each session opens with a time of prayer.

2. **Warm-up Question** – The purpose of the warm-up question is to introduce the Core Value through a real-life question that everyone can answer. Length: five to eight minutes.

3. **Testimonies** – Encourage personal testimony on how lives are being impacted through *Christian to the Core*. After session six, which teaches you how to share your personal story of following Christ, invite at least one person each week to share how they became a follower of Christ. Length: five minutes.

4. **Discussion** – This is the real heart of each session and should account for at least half of your total time together. The Discussion Guide will help you focus on the most important discussion questions. Be sensitive to the needs and interests of others in your group. Encourage broad participation.

5. **Application: Living Christian to the Core** – Each Core Value naturally leads to real-life, practical application. Consider specific actions each week to live out the Core Values.

6. **Closing Prayer** – Each session concludes with a time of prayer. The following suggestions are various ideas to help your group support each other through prayer:

   1. Collect requests each week, and have someone email them to the group.
   2. Have 3x5 index cards available for requests to be written down and exchanged.
   3. Divide participants into groups of two to four people, and allow eight to ten minutes to share specific needs and pray with each other.

Remember, the goal of this journey is personal transformation at the core or centre of your life. Therefore, practical application of the Core Values is essential.

Get Connected

Follow Us on Facebook and Twitter

"Like" us on Facebook at Facebook.com/ChristiantotheCore. Receive live updates by following us on Twitter at Twitter.com/Christian2Core.

Watch Us on Vimeo

Watch the latest inspirational and teaching videos at Vimeo.com/ILITeam.

Join the Christian to the Core Team

Visit ChristiantotheCore.org and click "Join" to receive email updates, new releases, links to inspirational videos, and more.

Visit Our Other Websites

To learn more about the International Leadership Institute (ILI), visit ILITeam.org. To explore ILI's global initiative for young leaders, visit History-Makers.org.

Connect with Our Offices

ILI Europe
K180
P.O. Box 26856
London
W7 2QJ
Web: www.k180.org
Email: c2c@k180.org

ILI USA
P.O. Box 1005
Carrollton, GA 30112
ILITeam@ILITeam.org

CHRISTIAN to the CORE

Table of Contents

The Core
Time-Tested Core Values for Christian Living

As the new millennium dawned, more than one-hundred Christian leaders from around the world gathered in Amsterdam to dream about the future and how they could impact the world for Christ. Everyone was inspired to believe that Habakkuk 1:5 was coming true in our days.

Look at the nations and watch—and be utterly amazed.
For I am going to do something in your days
that you would not believe, even if you were told.

After Amsterdam, global research was performed, and eight core values were discovered that described the most vibrant Christians. Curriculum was developed, and today, Christians around the world testify to the power of living by these eight core values.

Christian to the Core is a new resource designed to help you explore the Eight Core Values. This twelve-session journey will help you go deeper in your relationship with God, discover God's greater purposes for your life, and provide you with a stronger foundation to live the rest of your life.

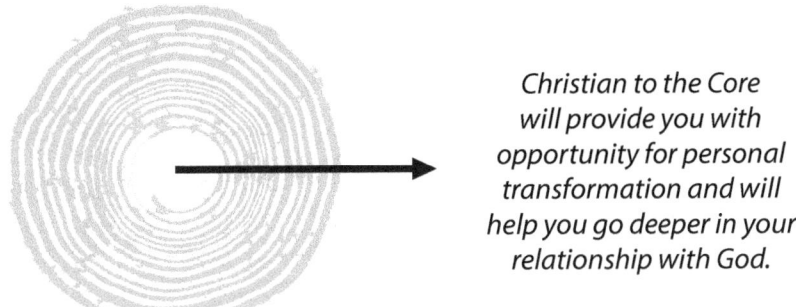

Christian to the Core will provide you with opportunity for personal transformation and will help you go deeper in your relationship with God.

What Are Your Expectations?

A sense of expectancy should be a part of every Christian's approach to life. When Jesus walked this earth, the crowds who followed him expected something to happen. For a Christian, expectancy and faith in God are closely related. In the New Testament, Hebrews 11:1 defines faith as "being sure of what we hope for and certain of what we do not see."

Faith in God results in an expectant hope for the future. *Christian to the Core* will provide you with relevant information and the opportunity for personal transformation. As you begin this journey, what are some of your expectations? Considering your current life situation, complete the following sentences:

I want to learn more about _____

I want to learn how to _____

I want my spiritual life to be different by _____

Intimacy
Passion
Vision
Evangelism
Multiplication
Family
Stewardship
Integrity

This session introduces the Eight Core Values so you may become familiar with the key check points along the journey. **What does the word "core" mean to you when applied to your life?**

Introduction to the Eight Core Values

1. Intimacy with God

God looks for consecrated men and women who live life from an intimate relationship with God.

Biblical Foundation — Exodus 33:9,11
As Moses went into the tent, the pillar of cloud would come down and stay at the entrance, while the LORD spoke with Moses…The LORD would speak to Moses face to face, as a man speaks with a friend.

The world needs people who are deep in their spiritual lives. True intimacy with God occurs through intentional effort over a long period of time as your relationship grows deeper.

What one thing could you do today to develop greater intimacy with God?

2. Passion for the Harvest

God looks for men and women who share a passion for those without Christ. In Luke 19:10, Jesus said he came to "seek and to save that which was lost." God desires that everyone be reached with the life-transforming power of the Gospel.

Biblical Foundation — Matthew 9:35-38
Jesus went through all the towns and villages, teaching in their synagogues, preaching the good news of the kingdom and healing every disease and sickness. When he saw the crowds, he had compassion on them, because they were harassed and helpless, like sheep without a shepherd. Then he said to his disciples, "The harvest is plentiful but the workers are few. Ask the LORD of the harvest, therefore, to send out workers into his harvest field."

Two-thirds of the world's population has not yet responded to God's love. Until all are reached with the Gospel, every Christian is challenged to accept the awesome opportunity to share the Good News with others.

Intimacy
Passion
Vision
Evangelism
Multiplication
Family
Stewardship
Integrity

Can you name someone in your life that needs to know God and his love? Would you pray for this person daily for the next thirty days?

3. The Power of Vision

God looks for men and women who discover God's vision for their lives, set goals, mobilise people, and overcome obstacles in order to see God's purposes achieved.

<u>Biblical Foundation</u> — Habakkuk 2:2 NASB
> *Then the LORD answered me and said, "Record the vision and inscribe it on tablets, that the one who reads it may run."*

God created you to be a person of purpose. Vision is God's tool to help you discover God's greater purposes for your life. Vision will help you establish life priorities, motivate your commitment, fuel your passion, and help you focus to reach your full potential in Christ.

Describe your best understanding of God's purpose or vision for your life.

4. Culturally Relevant Evangelism

God looks for men and women who live and share the Good News of Jesus Christ with cultural relevance, sensitivity, and power so that the eternal truth of the Gospel will be understood and received in every culture of the world.

<u>Biblical Foundation</u> — 1 Corinthians 9:19, 22b
> *Though I am free and belong to no one, I have made myself a slave to everyone, to win as many as possible.... I have become all things to all people so that by all possible means I might save some.*

The life-transforming power of the Gospel must be communicated with cultural relevance by word and deed in the power of the Holy Spirit. The Gospel is equally relevant to every language and culture in the world.

What are the best ways to share God's love with people in your environment?

Intimacy
Passion
Vision
Evangelism
Multiplication
Family
Stewardship
Integrity

NOTES

5. Multiplication of Disciples

God looks for men and women who disciple, coach, and mentor others, who in turn become effective disciple-makers.

Biblical Foundation — 2 Timothy 2:2
> *And the things you have heard me say in the presence of many witnesses entrust to reliable people who will also be qualified to teach others.*

God's main strategy to reach the world with the Gospel is through the multiplication of faithful disciples of Christ. Every Christian has the responsibility to multiply the impact of the Gospel in the lives of others by making disciples of Jesus.

Who is discipling you to follow Jesus? How could you help disciple someone to follow Jesus?

6. Family Priority

God looks for men and women who are convinced that the family is God's building block for society and give their family priority in their lives.

Biblical Foundation — Genesis 1:27-28
> *So God created man in his own image, in the image of God he created him; male and female he created them. God blessed them and said to them, "Be fruitful and increase in number; fill the earth and subdue it."*

God ordained the family and provides guidelines for developing healthy, strong families. Family is the first place that you should extend your love and influence.

What are the greatest opportunities and challenges facing your family right now?

Intimacy
Passion
Vision
Evangelism
Multiplication
Family
Stewardship
Integrity

7. Faithful Stewardship

God looks for men and women who are faithful stewards of finances, time, and spiritual gifts in their personal lives and in their service to God and others.

Biblical Foundation — Matthew 25:23
His master replied, "Well done, good and faithful servant! You have been faithful with a few things; I will put you in charge of many things. Come and share your master's happiness!"

Every follower of Christ is responsible for using God's gifts to achieve maximum impact for the Kingdom of God.

How are you using your finances, time, and spiritual gifts to bring the Kingdom of God on earth? Is there anything that you would like to do differently?

8. Integrity

God looks for men and women of integrity who live holy lives that are accountable to God and to the Body of Christ. Integrity glorifies God, protects us from stumbling, and encourages growth.

Biblical Foundation — 2 Timothy 4:7
I have fought the good fight, I have finished the race, I have kept the faith.

God desires that all Christians maintain integrity and finish well in their lives. Integrity provides moral authority for our lives.

How do you live your daily life with integrity?

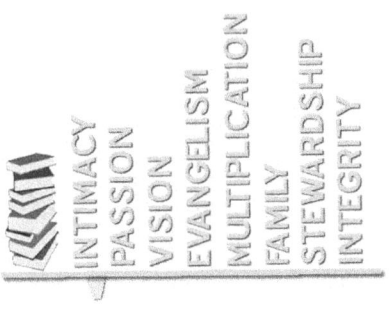

The Eight Core Values are like a bookshelf with the books listed in a special order. The two bookends are *Intimacy with God* and *Integrity*. In between are the other six Core Values. Each is critically important by itself; however, the real power and synergy of the Core Values come from balancing all eight in your life. With all eight, your life has strength and great satisfaction. Although you will face many challenges, you will be equipped to experience God's power and presence each day.

Intimacy
Passion
Vision
Evangelism
Multiplication
Family
Stewardship
Integrity

Application — Living Christian to the Core

All builders know that a strong foundation is essential for every building project. Any weak area will eventually compromise other parts of the building. When the foundation is strong, the building will endure for generations.

The Eight Core Values create a powerful foundation for living a meaningful and purposeful life. Each is essential, but the real strength is found in the way the Eight Core Values work together. They are the foundation for this journey; they are the foundation for your life. Compare them with your expectations, and evaluate your life based on the Eight Core Values.

Rank each of the statements below from 1 (strongly disagree) to 5 (strongly agree) by circling the appropriate number.

I have an intimate relationship with God

1 ———————— 2 ———————— 3 ———————— 4 ———————— 5

I possess God's passionate and sacrificial love for people.

1 ———————— 2 ———————— 3 ———————— 4 ———————— 5

I discovered God's purpose for my life, and I am living out that purpose.

1 ———————— 2 ———————— 3 ———————— 4 ———————— 5

I share God's love with people in the hope that they will become a follower of Jesus.

1 ———————— 2 ———————— 3 ———————— 4 ———————— 5

I am using my life to help others know God and experience the blessings of Christian life.

1 ———————— 2 ———————— 3 ———————— 4 ———————— 5

I exercise good stewardship over the time, money, and talents that God has given me.

1 ———————— 2 ———————— 3 ———————— 4 ———————— 5

My family is my first priority after my relationship with God.

1 ———————— 2 ———————— 3 ———————— 4 ———————— 5

I am committed to integrity in every area of my life and in all circumstances.

1 ———————— 2 ———————— 3 ———————— 4 ———————— 5

But seek first his Kingdom and his righteousness, and all these things will be given to you as well.

— Matthew 6:33

Prayer

Lord, as we explore the Eight Core Values, draw us into a deeper relationship with you. Help us to know the greater purposes you have for our lives. Build for us a strong foundation, and encourage us as we encourage one another to follow you. Amen.

Intimacy
Passion
Vision
Evangelism
Multiplication
Family
Stewardship
Integrity

Discussion Guide

1. In preparation for each week, study the session before coming to your small group. Write down your answers to the questions. This will help you to be engaged and grow as you hear the material for a second time.

2. Start the session with an opening prayer.

3. Begin each session with a warm-up question to help introduce the Core Value. For example: If you really want to know me, you need to know _____ about me.

4. The main goal of this first session is to get you acquainted with the ILI Eight Core Values and with other members of your group.

5. In the text of this session, a discussion question follows the introduction of each Core Value. Because each Core Value will be studied in detail in the following weeks, limit your discussion of each to five minutes or less so you have time to discuss all eight. We encourage you to share personal experiences and reflections.

6. IMPORTANT: The application exercise in this session is important to help you establish a beginning point for this journey. If you have not completed the exercise, do so during the session. Twelve sessions from now, you will revisit this exercise and discover where you have grown during the Christian to the Core journey.

7. End the session with a closing prayer.

Intimacy
Passion
Vision
Evangelism
Multiplication
Family
Stewardship
Integrity

Intimacy with God
Going Deeper

Core Value	God looks for consecrated men and women who live life from an intimate relationship with God.

In your mind, picture a place that is deep. Deep places can be fascinating.

Imagine you are on a boat over the Great Barrier Reef in Australia. When you look down on the reef, the image is blurry, but you know there are rock formations, coral, and fish beneath. You put on a mask and dive beneath the surface of the water. Instantly, you realise that you are in one of the most beautiful places on earth. You are awestruck by the variety of plant and animal life. Multi-coloured fish swim gently among a kaleidoscope of sea fans and coral. If you had not dived into the depths, you would have missed knowing the true beauty of this special place.

Now, imagine exploring a cave and travelling deep into the earth until you discover unusual rock formations. Perhaps you even find gorgeous gems such as quartz, amethysts, turquoise, rubies, or diamonds. If you go deep enough, you might even discover something no one else has ever seen.

In both examples, you only experience the beauty of the ocean reef or the majesty of a cave when you take the time to explore the depths. The same is true of our relationship with God. You can have a surface relationship, or you can go deeper and develop an intimate relationship with God and discover the inspiring depths and towering heights of his love.

The first Core Value is Intimacy with God. It serves as the foundation for every other aspect of our lives.

Some of God's best truths, like priceless treasures, are hidden in depths most people never take the time to explore.

Biblical Foundation — Knowing God

> *As Moses went into the tent, the pillar of cloud would come down and stay at the entrance, while the LORD spoke with Moses... The LORD would speak to Moses face to face, as a man speaks with his friend... — Exodus 33: 9,11*

The Bible is filled with images of God's desire for a personal relationship with individuals. In Exodus 33:7-12, we read of a powerful account of God meeting with Moses as he led the people toward the Promised Land.

Intimacy
Passion
Vision
Evangelism
Multiplication
Family
Stewardship
Integrity

Wherever the nation of Israel camped, a special tent served as a place where Moses would meet with God. Whenever Moses entered the tent, a cloud symbolising God's presence came down and stayed at the entrance. Moses came to meet God, and God came to meet Moses. When people saw the cloud, they remained at a distance and worshipped. Inside the tent, God spoke to Moses "face to face, as a man speaks with his friend."

"In the Garden" by C. Austin Miles is one of the most beloved hymns of the church. The chorus reads,

> *And he walks with me and he talks with me,*
> *and he tells me I am his own.*
> *And the joy we share as we tarry there,*
> *none other has ever known.*

God truly desires to walk with us and talk with us in our daily lives. Intimacy with God is a relationship in which you come to know God on a deep and personal level similar to the kind of relationship you might have with a best friend. God wants to know you, and he wants to be known by you. True friendship dispels fear and insecurity as friends share unconditional love and commitment. Moses' friendship with God was not a distant connection but a close, intimate, personal relationship.

In John 10:30, Jesus describes his intimate relationship with God the Father when he says, "I and the Father are one." Further, we discover in John 17:20–21 that Jesus prays for each of his followers to experience that same level of intimacy. Jesus prays,

> *Father, just as you are in me, and I am in you. May they also be in us.*

It is amazing to know that Jesus was praying for our relationship with God to be as deep as his relationship with his Father. Through the prophet Jeremiah, God spoke about intimacy with God when he said,

> *This is what the LORD says: "Let not the wise man boast of his wisdom or the strong man boast of his strength or the rich man boast of his riches, but let him who boasts boast about this: that he understands and knows me. . ." — Jeremiah 9:23-24*

Going Deeper: For further study, read Psalm 139:1-6.

Your Relationship With God

Describe your relationship with God. Is it as intimate as the connection you have with your best friend? Why or why not?

Pause to reflect for a moment. Are you ready and willing to go deeper in your relationship with God?

How does the Biblical account of God's relationship with Moses and Jesus encourage you to believe that God wants to know you and be known by you?

The Daily Challenge – Breaking Through the Four Barriers

We develop intimacy with God intentionally as we walk each day with God. The journey enriches us with moments of profound insight, life-transforming guidance, and personal experience of God's love. Yet this journey also involves significant challenges that can hinder or even block our relationship with God.

1. Superficiality and Shallowness

One challenge in contemporary culture is our satisfaction with superficiality and shallowness in life and relationships. Richard Foster offers the following commentary:

> Superficiality is the curse of our age. The doctrine of instant satisfaction is a primary spiritual problem. The desperate need today is not for a great number of intelligent people, or gifted people, but for deep people. [1]

How does Isaiah 29:13 describe "superficial"?

We must make time alone with God a priority each day.

2. Failure to Prioritise

Another challenge is overcoming the simple failure to prioritise. Many people can identify with the person who said, "I am lonely, shallow, and enslaved to a schedule that never lets up." The tyranny of the urgent can leave you running from deadline to deadline with little time for important relationships. Intimacy with God needs to become as necessary as the air you breathe or the water you drink.

In Psalm 42:1-2, how does the Psalmist describe his priority for God?

Intimacy
Passion
Vision
Evangelism
Multiplication
Family
Stewardship
Integrity

3. Focus on Information Instead of Intimacy

One can know a great deal about God without really knowing God. You can study Christian history, theology, and the creeds, you can even study the Bible, and yet you may not experience true intimacy with God. Knowledge about God is not the same as having a deep, personal relationship with God.

What characteristics did Paul describe in 2 Timothy 3:7?

Going Deeper: For further study, read I Timothy 2:4, 2 Timothy 2:25-26, and Titus 1:1-2.

4. Unconfessed Sins

A fourth challenge comes out of our moral failures and our disobedience. Unconfessed sin becomes an insurmountable barrier to intimacy with God. Sin separates us from God. Through Jesus Christ, however, we can have forgiveness of sins and a restored relationship with God.

How does the apostle John affirm this truth in 1 John 1:9?

Of the four barriers listed, which are hindering you from going deeper in your relationship with God?

How could you adjust your priorities to develop a greater intimacy with God?

Intimacy
Passion
Vision
Evangelism
Multiplication
Family
Stewardship
Integrity

Spiritual Disciplines – The Path for Intimacy with God

God provides every Christian with a simple path for experiencing God's grace and developing a more personal, intimate relationship. The path is found in spiritual disciplines, which include worship, Bible study, prayer, and service.

Spiritual disciplines are means of grace that move us beyond surface living and into the depths of spiritual reality. The primary requirement is a longing after God's heart. As in other areas of life, such as farming, athletics, and military training, discipline produces results. Disciplines are not negatives. They are positive opportunities for growth.

Worship	Bible Study	Prayer	Service

Worship

Worship occurs when we express our love to God with our whole selves. Throughout Scripture, whenever people worship, God reveals his glory among them. Worship involves your heart, mind, body, and spirit all actively loving and adoring Almighty God. Worship may also involve prayer, meditation, singing, listening, and responding to God's grace. Worship can be private, alone in your room, or in public while joining with others in a worship service. Through worship, you open your life to God, and he reveals himself to you.

According to Mark 12:30, what is a key element in worship?

Going Deeper: For further study, read 1 Chronicles 16:29, John 4:23-24, and Psalm 122:1.

Bible Study

No other book is like the Bible. Written over thousands of years by more than forty authors, the Bible is the world's best-selling book year after year and has been translated into more languages that any book in history. Grounded in human history, the Bible is special because it reveals who God is and how you can know him.

What does the Bible reveal about the nature of God in 2 Timothy 3:16-17?

Going Deeper: For further study, read Hebrews 4:12 and Psalm 19:7-11.

Prayer

Prayer is central to the life of a Christian because it brings us into direct communion with God. Real prayer is life-creating and life-changing. Prayer gives you the opportunity to express gratitude to God and also to share your needs and the needs of others. Through prayer, you communicate directly with God and learn to listen for God's special messages for your life.

Write out the special messages found in Philippians 4:6-7.

Going Deeper: For further study, read John 16:24 and Jeremiah 33:3.

Service

God created you with the capacity to love and serve. Through service, you become an instrument of God's grace and love in the lives of others. Jesus served and told us to serve. When you serve others and help meet their needs, you demonstrate that you are Christ's disciple. You also experience the power and presence of God in your life as you cooperate in helping to bring the Kingdom of God on earth.

> *Now that I, your Lord and Teacher, have washed your feet, you also should wash one another's feet. I have set you an example that you should do as I have done for you. — John 13:14-15*

Based on John 13:35, what identifies Christ's disciples?

Going Deeper: For further study, read Ephesians 2:10.

In addition to worship, Bible study, prayer, and service, you can use many other spiritual disciplines to cultivate your intimacy with God. Other practices such as journaling, memorising Scripture, physical exercise, fasting, silence, and tithing all serve to create a greater awareness of God's presence in your daily life. With all spiritual disciplines, the desired result is a deeper, more intimate relationship with God.

Intimacy
Passion
Vision
Evangelism
Multiplication
Family
Stewardship
Integrity

Application — Living Christian to the Core

God is looking for men and women who live life from an intimate relationship with God. To be Christian to the core is to have an intimate and growing relationship with the God of the universe. Just as God spoke to Moses face to face, he desires a personal relationship with you and has provided the pathway of spiritual disciplines to help you overcome any barriers to going deeper with him.

Consider your relationship with God. What can you do today to begin moving towards greater intimacy? Think about each of the four primary disciplines: worship, Bible study, prayer, service. **What can you do in each area to move more toward deeper intimacy?**

In worship I will. . .

In Bible study I will. . .

In prayer I will. . .

In service I will. . .

Before the next session, find a mature believer and discuss how he or she maintains a vibrant relationship with the Lord through worship, Scripture reading, prayer, and service. Based on the feedback you receive, write down three suggestions that will help you develop a more intimate relationship with God. Think of how you will apply these to your life.

Prayer

> *Almighty God, give me the strength and wisdom to prioritise my relationship with you. Help me spend time in quietness and reflection. Open my heart and speak to me. Take me deeper in my relationship with you so I might experience the fullness of your presence in my life.*

Intimacy
Passion
Vision
Evangelism
Multiplication
Family
Stewardship
Integrity

Discussion Guide

1. Start the session with an opening prayer.

2. Warm-up Question: The Core Value for this session will reflect on intimacy. Name a person with whom you feel close to and why?

3. Read the Core Value aloud at the beginning and end of the session together as a group.

4. For discussion, share your responses to the four barriers and what you need to do to overcome them.

5. Discuss each of the spiritual disciplines and note the benefits and challenges of each.

6. As you conclude the session, share what actions you will take to go deeper in your intimacy with God through worship, Bible, prayer, and service. If the group is large, break into groups of three and pray for one another.

7. End the session with a closing prayer.

Intimacy
Passion
Vision
Evangelism
Multiplication
Family
Stewardship
Integrity

16

Passion for the Harvest
Experiencing God's Passionate Heart for the Lost

Core Value	God looks for men and women who share a passion for those without Christ. Jesus came to "seek and to save that which was lost." God desires that everyone be reached with the life-transforming power of the Gospel.

The Bible tells the story of God's passionate love for people. His actions reveal his passion for those he has made. When he becomes flesh and takes centre stage in Jesus, we see a man relentless in the pursuit of others, including those who have been discounted, rejected, and despised.

A simple touch and the leper is healed. While others push lepers away, Jesus reaches out in love. A blind beggar cries out loudly as Jesus nears. The crowd tries to silence him, but Jesus stops to give him full attention and heals him too. Nicodemus, a religious leader with sincere questions, approaches Jesus at night. Jesus speaks straight to his heart, letting him know there is something more he needs – he needs to be born again. After Jesus' death, Nicodemus is the one who asks for his body and buries him.

Then there is the day when Jesus enters the temple courtyard, which is filled with money-grubbing marketers taking up all the space and displacing those who came to the temple to seek God. Jesus' passion rises to the surface. His love wants seekers to have access to God. He takes a whip, turns over tables, clears the courtyard and proclaims, "It is written 'My house will be called a house of prayer,' but you are making it a 'den of robbers.'"

Of course, God's ultimate heroic moment comes when Jesus allows himself to be betrayed into the hands of those who wanted him dead. After putting him through a show-trial, he is handed over to the brutal power of Rome to be hung on a cross until dead – the price to be paid for our sins. "Like a lamb led to the slaughter," he goes to his death, taking the sins of the world upon himself. Scripture reveals that God longs for people. Jesus gave his life so all people would know God's love. Now he invites us to share his passion and be his instrument of love to others.

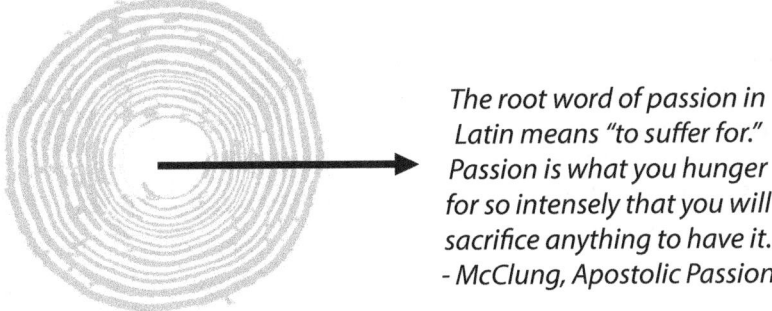

The root word of passion in Latin means "to suffer for." Passion is what you hunger for so intensely that you will sacrifice anything to have it.
- McClung, Apostolic Passion

Passion Defined

Passion is a force burning in you which seizes you and provides a power that moves you beyond ordinary human activity. Passion will not let you go until God's goals are reached. Passion is the fire and urgency that vision needs to remain alive and active.

Intimacy
Passion
Vision
Evangelism
Multiplication
Family
Stewardship
Integrity

Biblical Foundation

The Bible is full of individuals who embody God's passionate heart for others. Moses responded to God's call to lead his people out of slavery in Egypt. A young shepherd boy named David stood against a giant named Goliath who threatened God's people. A fisherman left his nets and extended God's offer of forgiveness to the very people who crucified Jesus. A Jewish nationalist changed his name to Paul and spent his life offering God's love to the nations he once despised.

Jeremiah was a young man, perhaps a teenager, when God filled him with his passion. To Jeremiah, passion was a fire that came from God and could not be extinguished.

> *But if I say, "I will not mention him or speak any more in his name," his word is in my heart like a fire, a fire shut up in my bones. I am weary of holding it in; indeed, I cannot. — Jeremiah 20:9*

Have you ever felt a passion that stirred you with a Jeremiah-like intensity? Describe that experience and what it felt like.

We are living in the time of the largest ingathering of people into the Kingdom of God that the world has ever seen.

— Patrick Johnstone, author of Operation World

Going Deeper: For further study, read about Paul's passion for the Jewish people in Romans 9-11.

Examples of Passion

God used John Wesley to bring revival and transform England. Today, 60 million people all over the world owe their spiritual heritage to this movement. Wesley exhorted his preachers,

> *Let us all be of one business. We live only for this, to save our own souls and the souls of those who hear us.* [1]

William Booth started the Salvation Army when his church turned a deaf ear to his plea to help the desperately poor in nineteenth-century London. The King of England asked Booth what the ruling force of his life was. Booth replied,

> *Sir, some men's passion is for gold, other men's passion is for fame, but my passion is for souls.* [2]

Much of the world knows Billy Graham as the greatest evangelist of the twentieth century. As a young man preaching to America's youth he wrote,

> *We are kindling a fire in this cold old world full of hatred and selfishness. Our little blaze may seem to be unavailing, but we must keep our fire burning.* [3]

Intimacy
Passion
Vision
Evangelism
Multiplication
Family
Stewardship
Integrity

18

Mother Theresa, founder of the Missionaries of Charity and winner of the Nobel Peace Prize, expressed deep passion for the lost when she said,

> *If I ever become a Saint—I will surely be one of "darkness." I will continually be absent from Heaven—to light the light of those in darkness on earth.*[4]

Passion for the Harvest

As you grow deeper in your relationship of intimacy with God, you will seek to be filled with more of his passion for others. In Luke 19:10, Jesus proclaims that he came to seek and to save that which was lost. God desires for everyone to be reached with the life-transforming power of the Gospel. Just as Jesus sought lost people when he walked on earth, still today he seeks the lost, and we are his messengers. Jesus' passion becomes our passion. He referred to those living without a relationship with God as "the harvest," ready to be gathered into the passionate love of the Father.

What does Jesus say about "the harvest" in John 4:35-36?

What did Jesus say to his disciples in Matthew 9:36-38 that would also apply to you?

The Global Challenge

We are living in one of the most exciting and yet challenging periods in God's salvation history. During the twentieth century, the world population multiplied 3.7 times. Yet, in Asia there are 15 times more Christians than 100 years ago, and in Africa, there are 38 times more Christians. However, the percentage of Christians in North America has remained about the same, while the number of Christians in Europe has not kept pace with the population, growing only 1.5 times. In Latin America, thousands are coming to Christ every day.

In Matthew 28:19, Jesus commanded all Christians to "go and make disciples." He instructed us to carry the Good News to every person in every culture, beginning across the street and going to the ends of the earth.

The population of Planet Earth is over seven billion people. The Church has been in existence and sharing the Good News of Christ for two-thousand years. Yet, two-thirds of the global population has yet to make a decision about the claims of the Gospel. Currently, the global challenge looks like this:

Intimacy
Passion
Vision
Evangelism
Multiplication
Family
Stewardship
Integrity

The Challenge to "Seek and Save the Lost" (Luke 19:9-10)

- More than two billion people are followers of Christ, a figure that includes all the different Christian denominations and groups. These people are saying, "Thank you, Jesus." They have a Bible in their language, a local church to attend, and a commitment to Jesus.

- More than two billion people are non-Christians who have access to the Gospel. They live where they can hear, learn, and respond to the Gospel, but they are not yet following Christ. These people are saying, "No thank you, Jesus."

- Almost two billion people remain unreached. They have little or no access to the Gospel. There have no Christian influence in their lives, no churches in their areas, and usually no Bibles in their languages. These people are saying, "Who is Jesus?"

The Challenge to Meet Practical Human Needs

In Matthew 25:31-46, Jesus calls his followers to action through his command to passionately meet the needs of others. In this powerful passage, the Lord comes to judge the nations by separating the sheep, or the faithful, from the goats, those found faithless. The faithful respond to the needs of people and are gathered up into glory. The faithless ignore the needs and experience some of the strongest language of judgment in the Bible. We live in a world of pressing need. God expresses his passion for those in need through the actions of those willing to respond in the name of Christ.

> Then the King will say to those on his right, "Come, you who are blessed of My Father, inherit the Kingdom prepared for you from the foundation of the world. For I was hungry, and you gave me something to eat; I was thirsty, and you gave me something to drink; I was a stranger, and you invited me in; naked, and you clothed me; I was sick, and you visited me; I was in prison, and you came to me." — Matthew 25:34-36

I Was Hungry and Thirsty	Approximately 850 million people across the world are hungry. Every five seconds, one child dies from hunger-related causes. Approximately one in every eight people lack access to safe water supplies, resulting in easily preventable diseases.[5]
I Was Naked	Approximately 2.7 billion people in the world live on less than $2 a day. More than 385 million human beings have to survive on less than $1 a day.[6]
I Was in Prison	More than 9.8 million people around the world are in prison, where they struggle with loneliness, rejection, and the cost of their crimes. In addition, many Christians have been unjustly imprisoned for their faith. In one nation, more than 3,000 Christians have been jailed during the last decade. In addition to imprisonment, more Christians were martyred in the twentieth century than in the previous nineteen.[7]
I Was Sick	Malaria is the leading cause of death and illness worldwide. Dysentery, which is easily preventable by simple sanitation, continues to kill 1.4 million children every year. More than 30.8 million adults and 2 million children live with HIV. In the year 2009, more than 2.7 million people became infected with this virus.[8]

Intimacy
Passion
Vision
Evangelism
Multiplication
Family
Stewardship
Integrity

The Spiritual Challenge in the UK[9]

The Church faces significant spiritual challenges. Most mainline denominations are declining, and population is increasingly secular. There are outstanding churches and ministries in the UK who are effectively making disciples; however, the following facts must be faced:

1. In the 10 years from 1998 to 2008, belief in God dropped from 68% to 54% of the population.[9] This trend is confirmed by the 2011 UK Census, where respondents stating they had "no religion" rose from 14.8% in 2001 to 25.1% in 2011.[10]

2. In 2011, 88% of adults did not know the details of the Christmas story.[9]

3. In 2010, church attendance was 32% lower than it was in 1990 with the sharpest decline being in the "under 15" bracket, closely followed by the "15-29" age bracket.[11] This trend is confirmed by the 2011 UK Census, where those respondents identifying themselves as "Christian" decreased from 71.1% in 2001 to 59.3% in 2011.[10]

4. In the 5 years from 2005 to 2010, 1,230 churches opened, whilst 1350 closed.[11]

For those born before 1946	65% professed Christ
For those born between 1946 and 1964	35% professed Christ
For those born between 1965 and 1976	15% professed Christ

   Do you detect a trend? Here comes the reality check.

For those born between 1976 and 1994	4% professed Christ [13]

5. The UK has seen a steady decline in workers being sent into the mission field. If current trends continue, it will not be long before the UK will soon be receiving more missionaries than sending them.[11]

Read how Jesus responded to these challenges in Matthew 9:36-38. **How do you respond to the Global and UK challenge?**

How God's Passion Becomes Our Passion

Although the challenges are great, we know that all things are possible through him who strengthens us (Philippians 4:13). Our intimate walk with God leads to his heart and passion for the lost. God's passion becomes our passion. Consider the following three key facts about passion:

1. Passion is the direct result of our love for Christ and our commitment to Him.

> *For Christ's love compels us, because we are convinced that one died for all, and therefore all died. And he died for all, that those who live should no longer live for themselves, but for him who died for them and was raised again. — 2 Corinthians 5:14-15*

Intimacy
Passion
Vision
Evangelism
Multiplication
Family
Stewardship
Integrity

In his devotional, *My Utmost for His Highest,* Oswald Chambers states, "The passion of Christianity comes from deliberately signing away our rights and becoming a bondservant of Jesus Christ."

Going Deeper: For further study, go online and search the word "bondservant." Reflect on how this is different from a regular servant.

2. Passion Must be Nurtured.

As God feeds and nurtures our soul through spiritual disciplines and his presence, our passion increases and sustains our vision. Passion must be nurtured and maintained like a fire. Just as our intimacy must be continually rekindled, so must our passion. Vision relates directly to passion. When passion decreases, vision also becomes more distant and dim.

What did Paul urge Timothy to do in 2 Timothy 1:6-7 and for what reason?

3. Passion Comes from God.

Wesley Duewel writes in *Ablaze for God*

We cannot light this fire. In ourselves we cannot produce it.
No man can kindle in himself that celestial fire;
it must come from the coal from the altar above.

From Matthew 7:7-8 write out the three steps that will enable you to fully experience God's passion for the harvest.

Intimacy
Passion
Vision
Evangelism
Multiplication
Family
Stewardship
Integrity

22

Application — Living Christian to the Core

God looks for men and women who share a passion for those without Christ. God desires for everyone to be reached with the life-transforming power of the Gospel.

Healthy Christians share their faith in word and deed. Living Christian to the core means that you share God's love in word and deed. The needs of the world can seem overwhelming; however, as God's love and passion for others fills your heart, you will be empowered to share God's love with lost and hurting people so they, too, can be transformed by God's love through Jesus Christ.

To be filled with God's passionate love for others, Jesus calls us to ask, to seek, and to knock. His passion comes only with a persistent pursuit of his heart. Too many people drift in the easy currents of self-satisfaction and comfort, while yearning for a life filled with passion. Ask for his fullness. Seek his presence. Knock until he opens to you his most precious possession: his passion for the lost.

Your Prayer for God's Passion

God, I want the passion that you have for the lost to become my passion. I ask that from on high you send fire into my bones just as you did to Jeremiah. Let this fire burn away anything that is keeping me from experiencing your divine passion. Following the example of your passionate Son, I want to "seek the lost" and help others become followers of Christ.

In Jesus' name I pray,

Amen

Your Signature _____

Today's Date _____

Intimacy
Passion
Vision
Evangelism
Multiplication
Family
Stewardship
Integrity

Discussion Guide

1. **Start the session with an opening prayer.**

2. **Warm-up Question: How would you describe someone that you consider passionate? How does their passion make you feel?**

3. **Read the Core Value aloud at the beginning and end of the session together as a group.**

4. **Following the introduction and definitions, read the quote by McClung. Is this is how you understand the meaning of passion?**

5. **Allow time for responses to the question: Have you ever felt a passion that stirred you with a Jeremiah-like intensity? Describe that experience and what it felt like. If time permits, also look up Acts 4:18-20 and Galatians 2:20 to read about the passion of Peter and Paul.**

6. **Read aloud the statistics by Patrick Johnstone in "The Global Challenge." Give your thoughts on why the church is growing in places *other* than Europe.**

7. **What is Jesus wanting us to understand from John 4:35-36 (the fields are ripe) and Matthew 9:36-38 (the workers are few)?**

8. **Review and discuss the three principles for "How God's Passion Becomes Our Passion."**

9. **Read the closing prayer together. Sign the prayer for God's passion if you have not already done so.**

Intimacy
Passion
Vision
Evangelism
Multiplication
Family
Stewardship
Integrity

24

The Power of Vision

Knowing God's Vision for Your Life

Core Value	God looks for men and women who discover God's vision for their lives, set goals, mobilise people, and overcome obstacles in order to see God's purposes achieved.

A blind person's world is bounded by the limits of his or her touch; an ignorant person's world by the limits of his or her knowledge; a great person's by the limits of his or her vision. — E. Paul Hovey

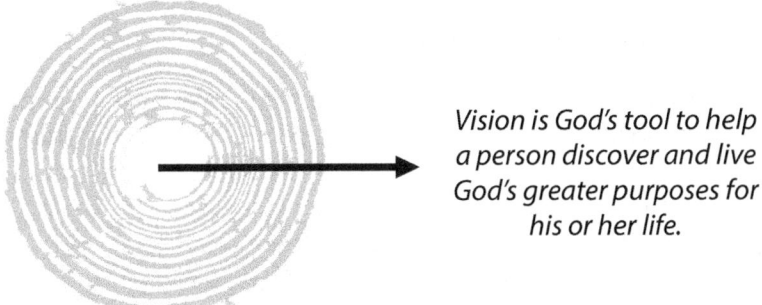

Vision is God's tool to help a person discover and live God's greater purposes for his or her life.

God created us to be people of purpose, and vision is God's tool to help every Christian live from the core of his or her being. There are many definitions of vision. One of the most helpful is from Bill Hybels, the senior pastor of the Willow Creek Church and the global Willow Creek Fellowship movement. He writes,

Vision is a picture of the future that produces passion. [1]

Do you have a clear sense of God's purpose, or vision, for your life? How would you describe it?

Vision is so powerful that it will clarify your life purpose, help you establish clear priorities, set standards of excellence, inspire expectation, motivate commitment, maximise productivity, expand your horizons, fuel passion, and provide focus for reaching your fullest potential.

Intimacy
Passion
Vision
Evangelism
Multiplication
Family
Stewardship
Integrity

What Is Vision Like?

Vision is like the Eye of the Eagle

An eagle sees farther than any other animal. In the same way, vision allows you to look into the future and see a life filled with purpose and meaning.

Vision is like a Magnifying Glass

A magnifying glass brings objects into clearer focus. Vision from God allows you to see your life with greater clarity and focus.

Vision is like the Banks of a River

The banks of a river provide direction for the flow of the water. Vision provides direction and keeps you moving in the direction that God wants you to go.

Do You Know God's Vision for Your Life?

You are special, unique, and created for a purpose; discovering that purpose is one of the great joys of the Christian life. **Where are you in the process of discovering your vision?**

_____ I am clueless.
_____ I have some ideas but need clarity.
_____ I know God's vision for life, and I am pursuing it.

Can you envision a future so appealing that you are willing to partner with God to see that future created? Can you describe it?

Discovering God's Vision for Your Life — Lessons from Nehemiah

God can choose to reveal his vision for your life through a supernatural experience like a dream in the night or divine visitation from an angel. For most people, however, the process God uses to reveal vision is less dramatic, yet completely life-transforming. It begins when you see a particular need, and it becomes clear when you realise that God is calling you to meet that need. God designed you for a purpose, and your purpose includes helping to meet needs on earth. To understand the process of how God births vision in the life of Christians, we will study Nehemiah, the cupbearer and personal servant to a Babylonian king. God used Nehemiah to change human history.

Intimacy
Passion
Vision
Evangelism
Multiplication
Family
Stewardship
Integrity

26

Historical Background

In 586 B.C. the Babylonians, under King Nebuchadnezzar, captured the city of Jerusalem, burned the house of God (the temple), broke down the protective wall, destroyed the city's valuable articles, and stole the national treasures.

The Jewish people were captured, forced into slavery, and marched almost 900 miles to Babylon, which is in modern day Iraq. Psalm 137:4 was written at this time, "How can we sing the songs of the LORD while in a foreign land?" For 70 years, the Jewish people lived in captivity. Then, God began to restore Jerusalem through three people: Zerubbabel, Ezra, and Nehemiah. Nehemiah's special call was to rebuild the walls of Jerusalem and restore security to the city.

As the book of Nehemiah begins, Nehemiah is serving as the cupbearer to the king, and he is about to learn God's vision for his life.

Going Deeper: For further study, read more about this historical account in 2 Kings 24:10-20.

When you find God's vision for your life, you will not take hold of it; it will take hold of you.

Five Steps in the Birth of Vision

God designed us to be people of purpose – to pursue causes for which we would exchange our lives. When you find God's vision for your life, you will not take hold of it; it will take hold of you. It will begin quietly as you encounter a particular need. There are five steps in the birth of vision:

1. See the Need

Nehemiah was deeply concerned about the Jewish people and the situation in Jerusalem. As the book of Nehemiah opens, he receives an update,

> *The words of Nehemiah the son of Hakaliah: In the month of Kislev in the twentieth year, while I was in the citadel of Susa, Hanani, one of my brothers, came from Judah with some other men, and I questioned them about the Jewish remnant that survived the exile, and also about Jerusalem. They said to me, "Those who survived the exile and are back in the province are in great trouble and disgrace. The wall of Jerusalem is broken down, and its gates have been burned with fire."*
> — *Nehemiah 1:1-3*

List the needs that were in Jerusalem based on the verses above.

Vision is normally

• *Birthed in human experience*

• *Based upon a human need*

Intimacy
Passion
Vision
Evangelism
Multiplication
Family
Stewardship
Integrity

God's vision for your life begins when you catch sight of a human plight that stirs you and touches a spiritual nerve. Quietly you experience the first step. This is the seeding process. Verse three is the answer to the question on Nehemiah's heart. As he hears the words, he visualizes the situation in Jerusalem. He has never actually been to Jerusalem, but he can see the city in his mind. He can see the people living in fear and uncertainty; he can see the broken walls. His emotions are touched.

The normal response to pain, suffering, and problems is to move away from them.

However, if God is birthing vision in your life, you are willing to intentionally put the need in your heart and even feel the pain personally.

2. Feel the Need

First you see the need. Then you feel the need. You begin to purposefully open your heart and allow the need inside of you. Another person's need becomes your own, and the seeds of vision begin to grow within your heart. Although many people see needs, there are times when seeds give birth to something deep in your heart with staying power. The need has leapt onto you, and now goes wherever you go. There is almost a chemical reaction between the need and the way God made you.

The news of Jerusalem's distress deeply impacted Nehemiah. It was exactly the opposite of what he hoped to hear. It affected him emotionally, and he sat down and wept. His heart broke for Jerusalem and the situation the people were facing.

In Nehemiah 1:4a, how was Nehemiah affected by what he heard? Have you ever experienced a need that touched you deeply and, perhaps, made you weep? Describe that experience.

3. Burden for the Need

The awareness of the need grows strong inside of you. The feelings do not leave. In fact, the feelings increase. At some point, you cross the line from objective observation to a soulful yearning that something must be done. You mourn for what you have seen. The burden weighs heavily, and you cannot escape it.

At this point in the process, God is bonding you as a chosen servant to help meet a need and bring the Kingdom of God on earth.

How did Nehemiah express his burden for the need in Nehemiah 1:4b?

Burdens

- *Birth great visions*

- *Provide passion for the vision*

Intimacy
Passion
Vision
Evangelism
Multiplication
Family
Stewardship
Integrity

What Would You Attempt for God?

Do you have a clear sense of a need that you could meet if God was with you? What would you attempt if you knew it would not fail?

Going Deeper: For further study, read Esther 4:4-12, and discover why Esther was told, "And who knows but that you have come to your royal position for such a time as this?"

4. Believe You Can Meet the Need

You could step out to meet the need, but will you? You are at a critical point. If this is a true vision struggling to be born, you have an internal accountability for the need. You feel a sense of responsibility and urgency to do something. Softly wrapped around the burden, is the quiet persistent confidence that you are being called by God to take action.

This step will validate your accountability to God and people. It will also require you to:

- Be obedient
- Act in faith
- Acknowledge the power of God

5. Take Action to Meet the Need

You have seen and felt a need. God has laid upon your heart a burden for this need, and now you know that you must take action to meet the need. Where do you begin?

Great action plans begin with developing clear goals that are specific, measurable, attainable by faith, realistic, and time targeted. In the English language, the first letter of each of these principles spells the word **SMART**.

S pecific

M easurable

A ttainable

R ealistic

T ime Targeted

What was Nehemiah's plan of action in Nehemiah 2:4-5?

If you don't know where you are going, any road can lead to your destination.

— Anonymous

Intimacy
Passion
Vision
Evangelism
Multiplication
Family
Stewardship
Integrity

Goals provide a clear strategy and action plan. When you act upon a vision that God has placed upon your life, you will acknowledge the power of God and validate your accountability to God and people. Your action will require a step of faith involving risk, and it will launch you into a more dynamic and exciting relationship with God as you pursue his vision for your life.

Application — Living Christian to the Core

A special prophet of God, named Habakkuk, wrote these words on the importance of vision:

> Then the Lord answered me and said, "Record the vision and inscribe it on tablets, that the one who reads it may run." — Habakkuk 2:2

Nehemiah discovered God's vision and ran with it. The walls had been torn down for more than one hundred and fifty years. Being the cupbearer to the king, Nehemiah had no authority over his life and no financial resources; yet, when he discovered God's vision for his life, he set goals, mobilised people, and overcame obstacles until the walls of Jerusalem were rebuilt and security was restored. And, it only took fifty-two days to complete the work.

> So the wall was completed on the twenty-fifth of Elul, in fifty-two days. When all our enemies heard about this, all the surrounding nations were afraid and lost their self-confidence, because they realised this work had been done with the help of our God. — Nehemiah 6:15-16

One man, following God's vision, changed history.

What have you learned about God's vision for your life in this session?

What is your best understanding of God's vision or purpose for your life?

So the wall was completed on the twenty-fifth of the month of Elul, in fifty-two days.

— Nehemiah 6:15

Intimacy
Passion
Vision
Evangelism
Multiplication
Family
Stewardship
Integrity

If you are struggling to know God's vision for your life, then write a list of needs that you see which touch your emotions. What action could you take this week to explore God's vision for your life?

If you already know God's vision for your life, what SMART goal can you set and take action upon this week to make a significant step toward fulfilling that vision?

History is different and many lives were changed because Nehemiah was faithful to God's vision for his life. Be encouraged. Seek God's plan for your life. Take action, and you will also be a history maker.

Prayer

> *Almighty God, thank you for designing us to be people of purpose who can meet the needs of other people and the needs of the world by following your vision for our lives. Give us compassion for others and the courage to take action.*

Intimacy
Passion
Vision
Evangelism
Multiplication
Family
Stewardship
Integrity

31

Discussion Guide

1. Start the session with an opening prayer.

2. Warm-up Question: When you hear the word "vision," what thought first comes to your mind?

3. Read the Core Value aloud at the beginning and end of the session together as a group.

4. In the section titled "Historical Background," have someone tell the story of Nehemiah.

5. In the section titled "Five Steps in the Birth of Vision," in Step One, discuss the importance of a vision being based on someone else's need and not your own.

6. In the section titled "Five Steps in the Birth of Vision," in Step Two, share a story about a need you saw that touched you deeply.

7. In the section titled "Five Steps in the Birth of Vision," in Step Four, share something you would attempt for God if you knew it would not fail.

8. Share your action plan according to the SMART principles found in the section titled "Take Action to Meet the Need."

9. End the session with a closing prayer.

Intimacy
Passion
Vision
Evangelism
Multiplication
Family
Stewardship
Integrity

32

Overcoming Obstacles
Finding Strength in Christ

Core Value	God looks for men and women who discover God's vision, set goals, mobilize people, and overcome obstacles in order to achieve God's purposes.

Personal transformation is one of the marks of the Christian life; however, it is a myth that problems and obstacles disappear because you are a Christian. The difference is that followers of Christ have the Spirit of God at work in their lives as various challenges arise. Jesus understood this principle and said,

> *I have told you these things, so that in me you may have peace. In this world you will have trouble. But take heart! I have overcome the world.*
> — *John 16:33*

Jesus was guided by a divine vision for his life. Yet, he also faced many obstacles. His life provides an example for overcoming obstacles in our own lives.

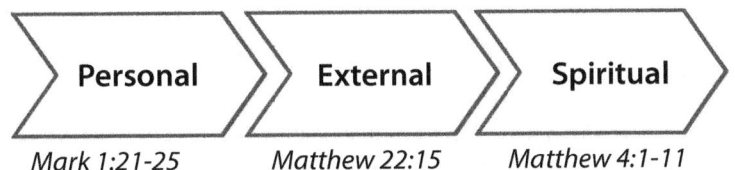

Personal	External	Spiritual
Mark 1:21-25	*Matthew 22:15*	*Matthew 4:1-11*

Jesus shared our humanity and, consequently, faced obstacles we are confronted with in our daily life. He experienced **personal** obstacles, like rejection and loneliness when his family and closest friends did not understand him and his synagogue rejected him.

Other obstacles were **external**. Some people challenged his teachings, questioned his growing influence, and undermined his popularity.

Finally, some obstacles were **spiritual**. Jesus faced spiritual warfare, including the devil himself. Evil is a reality in the world that we must learn to overcome. In the face of obstacles, Jesus overcame by completely relying on God. He experienced victory and continued toward fulfilling God's divine purpose for his life.

...Greater is he that is in you, than he that is in the world.

— 1 John 4:4b KJV

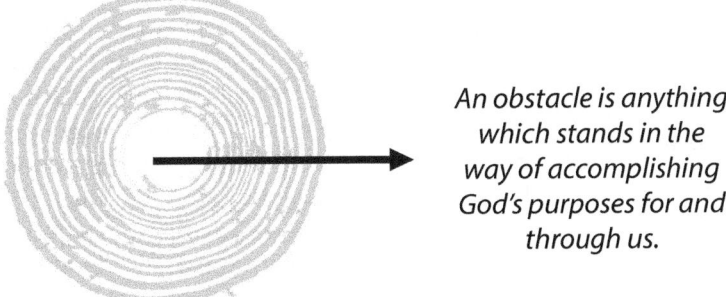

An obstacle is anything which stands in the way of accomplishing God's purposes for and through us.

Intimacy
Passion
Vision
Evangelism
Multiplication
Family
Stewardship
Integrity

Biblical Foundation — We Are More Than Conquerors

Who shall separate us from the love of Christ? Shall trouble or hardship or persecution or famine or nakedness or danger or sword? As it is written, "For your sake we face death all day long; we are considered as sheep to be slaughtered." No, in all these things we are more than conquerors through him who loved us. For I am convinced that neither death nor life, neither angels nor demons, neither the present nor the future, nor any powers, neither height nor depth, nor anything else in all creation, will be able to separate us from the love of God that is in Christ Jesus our Lord. — Romans 8:35-39

Diagnosed with cancer in the morning, I spent the rest of the day visiting doctors. That night, God reminded me that "nothing would separate me from the love of God." In that moment, God filled me fresh with the Holy Spirit to face a health obstacle. Through grace and a long struggle, my health is completely restored.

– Wes Griffin Co-founder, International Leadership Institute

This powerful Scripture puts obstacles into perspective and provides reassuring words regarding our struggles. Because of God's persistent love, we are more than conquerors through Christ.

Obstacles are a reality.	**No obstacle will ever separate us from the love of God, whether personal, external, or spiritual.**	**It is in the midst of the obstacles that we become more than conquerors through Christ.**

Overcoming Your Obstacles

Reflecting on your life, make a list of the challenges, problems, or obstacles you currently face. **What is the number one obstacle you would like to overcome?**

Personal

Personal obstacles are often experienced as inner struggles and limitations. These may be the most difficult to overcome because they are not always visible. Examples include moral obstacles, educational obstacles, medical obstacles, and emotional obstacles. One of the most challenging personal obstacles can be a poor view of oneself. When we fail to draw our sense of self-worth from God, we are unable to become the person God has created us to be. A right understanding of who we are in Christ transforms our own sense of self.

Intimacy
Passion
Vision
Evangelism
Multiplication
Family
Stewardship
Integrity

My Self-Image

Scripture affirms the importance of self-image. At times, we may feel like our greatest enemy is the mirror. We see ourselves through our own eyes rather than looking through the eyes of God.

For as [a man] thinks within himself, so he is. — Proverbs 23:7 NASB

Moses and Jeremiah are surprising examples of people in the Bible who felt unable to accomplish that which God had called them to do. Nevertheless, God used both of them to change history. Moses led the Hebrews out of Egypt and brought the world the Ten Commandments. Jeremiah warned Judah of coming judgment, yet prophesied God's restoration, sustaining the exiled nation with hope.

When God called these two men, they doubted themselves and their ability. Moses felt incompetent (Exodus 3-4), and Jeremiah thought he was too young and inexperienced (Jeremiah 1). Both men came to see themselves in relation to God and God's vision for their lives, rather than their own view of their pasts and limitations.

What led Moses and Jeremiah to go beyond the views they had of themselves to act on what God saw? Can it be the same for you?

Going Deeper: For further study, read about Moses and his insecurities in Exodus 3-4. To learn more about Jeremiah, read Jeremiah 1.

How Do You View Yourself?

Aspects of our past, such as learned behaviours, past sins, and poisoned relationships, can shape how we view ourselves and hinder our grasp of how God sees us. **What parts of your past hold you back from seeing yourself as God sees you?**

I've had more trouble with D. L. Moody than any man alive.

– D. L. Moody, Evangelist Founder of Moody Bible Institute

Intimacy
Passion
Vision
Evangelism
Multiplication
Family
Stewardship
Integrity

How God Views Us

God creates each person as valuable. Because of this value, we should work to establish a healthy self-image based on our identity in Christ. Psalm 139 reminds us that God creates each person as unique and valuable. He planned for us long before the world began, and he knit us together in our mother's womb. The Psalmist says in verse 14, "I will praise you, for I am fearfully and wonderfully made. Marvellous are your works..."

Ken Boa, writes in his book *Conformed to His Image,*

> *We cannot truly know ourselves unless we know our God. The only secure, stable, significant, and satisfying basis for self-identity is the reality of our new identification with Christ... In Christ we have been transferred out of the line of Adam and into the line of Christ. And in Christ we have a new dignity and purpose.* [1]

Your Identity in Christ

> *You were taught, with regard to your former way of life, to put off your old self, which is being corrupted by its deceitful desires; to be made new in the attitude of your minds; and to put on the new self, created to be like God in true righteousness and holiness.* — Ephesians 4:22-24

Because of what Christ did for us, we can have a clear sense of:

— Belonging and being loved

— Worth and value

— Being competent

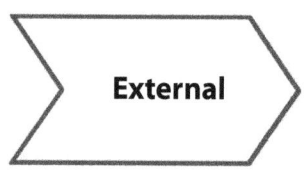 **External**

External obstacles develop from outside of ourselves. We are not the cause, but we must respond. External obstacles can arise from your church, workplace, family, community, neighbours, or even your nation. Many of these obstacles are associated with the relationships we encounter daily, and as a result, conflicts can occur. When conflict takes place, you need God's wisdom and guidance to heal and restore relationships as much as possible.

Steps to Resolve Conflict

Conflict may seem unavoidable when people are involved. It is important to handle any conflict in constructive ways. The following steps can guide you as you attempt to resolve conflict:

1. Examine yourself and understand the nature of the conflict. Appreciate differences in opinion.

2. Pray for wisdom to discern the actual issues and needs of those with whom you are in conflict. It is important to remember that the conflict may be about individual personalities and needs rather than the subject matter itself. Praying together can be an essential means of resolving a conflict.

Intimacy
Passion
Vision
Evangelism
Multiplication
Family
Stewardship
Integrity

3. Explore solutions together. When possible, attempt a win-win solution.

NOTES

LOSE-LOSE	Poorly managed conflict situations can lead to breakdown of relationships in which everyone loses.
WIN-LOSE	In a conflict situation, each time there is a winner, someone loses. Win-lose solutions should not be the norm.
WIN-WIN	The best possible solution comes with a mutual compromise in which everyone wins and foregoes something.

4. Make peace with others if you are in conflict. A common mistake is to confuse the issues in the conflict with the person, thus turning the conflict into a personal problem.

Win-Win Solutions

Think about a conflict that did not end well with a family member, friend, pastor, church member, employer, or employee. **Reflecting on the steps to resolve conflict, as well as the scripture mentioned, what could you have done differently to reach a "win–win" solution?**

Bless those who persecute you; bless and do not curse... Live in harmony with one another... Do not repay anyone evil for evil... If it is possible, as far as it depends on you, live at peace with everyone ... Do not be overcome by evil, but overcome evil with good.

— Romans 12:14, 16-18, 21

> **Spiritual**

Though we confront personal and external obstacles in different ways, the reality is that Satan is the source of all obstacles. Jesus told us in John 10:10 that the thief (the devil) "comes only to steal and kill and destroy" the people of God. In *Run with the Horses*, Eugene H. Peterson writes,

> *There is a spiritual war in progress, an all-out moral battle. There is evil and cruelty, unhappiness and illness. There is superstition and ignorance, brutality and pain. God is in continuous and energetic battle against all of it. There is no neutral ground in the universe. Every square foot of space is contested... No one enters existence as a spectator.* [2]

If it has blood, it is not your enemy.

Satan often tries to convince Christians that spiritual warfare is only about destroying idols and casting out demons. Although these activities are involved, spiritual warfare is actually much more. The more intimate we become with God, the more intensely we will experience evil attacks. The important fact is that God understands who the enemy is, and he has provided us with everything we need to fight the good fight and be victorious.

Intimacy
Passion
Vision
Evangelism
Multiplication
Family
Stewardship
Integrity

Biblical Perspective — You Are Provided with the Armour of God

Finally, be strong in the Lord and in his mighty power. Put on the full armour of God so that you can take your stand against the devil's schemes. For our struggle in not against the flesh and blood, but against the rulers, against the authorities, against the powers of this dark world, and against the spiritual forces of evil in the heavenly realms. Therefore put on the full armour of God, so that when the day of evil comes, you may be able to stand your ground, and after you have done everything, to stand. Stand firm then, with the belt of truth buckled around your waist, with the breastplate of righteousness in place, and with your feet fitted with the readiness that comes from the Gospel of peace. In addition to all this, take up the shield of faith, with which you can extinguish all the flaming arrows of the evil one. Take the helmet of salvation and the sword of the Spirit, which is the word of God. And pray in the Spirit on all occasions with all kinds of prayers and requests. With this in mind, be alert and always keep on praying for all the saints. — Ephesians 6:10-18

Going Deeper: For further study, read 2 Corinthians 11:26-28, Acts 6:1-7, 1 Corinthians 3:1-4, and Mark 6:5.

Your Armour

God provides you with spiritual armour so you can stand strong in your life. Review the list in Ephesians 6:14-18.

How does this Scripture help you stand strong and overcome spiritual obstacles?

Intimacy
Passion
Vision
Evangelism
Multiplication
Family
Stewardship
Integrity

38

Application — Living Christian to the Core

For though we live in the world, we do not wage war as the world does. The weapons we fight with are not the weapons of the world. On the contrary, they have divine power to demolish strongholds.
— 2 Corinthians 10:3-4

As we live and serve Christ in his Kingdom, obstacles will come. The statement, "it is not a question of if, but when" seems dauntingly true when applied to spiritual warfare of the Christian life. The experience of personal, external, and spiritual obstacles can be overwhelming, especially when two or three obstacles happen at a one time. How we overcome these obstacles can be defining moments in our life.

Developing practical ideas ahead of the battle can help clarify the best methods for overcoming each obstacle. **What strategies can you identify to help you overcome the various obstacles you encounter? Identify strategies for each area, both for smaller struggles and for the more difficult ones.** Be ready to discuss how these ideas may help you "be more than a conqueror through him who loves us."

Personal:

External:

Spiritual:

Jesus often used the Word of God to overcome the obstacles he encountered. Select a Scripture from this session or another location in the Bible and commit it to memory to help you overcome obstacles.

James Hudson Taylor founded the China Inland Mission in 1865 and was one of God's great Christian servants. He understood God's vision for his life; nevertheless, he experienced many personal, external, and spiritual obstacles. Commenting on the challenge to live the Christian life to the core, he stated,

> ### *First, it is impossible, then it is difficult, then it is done.* [3]

By the power of the Holy Spirit working in your life, you have access to every resource that you need to overcome obstacles and be "more than a conqueror" in Christ.

Prayer

Dear God, there are no obstacles we confront in our lives that you have not already confronted. You have given us the wisdom and weapons to be able to stand firm and overcome each obstacle. May we simply follow in your footsteps with our hearts totally focused on you, our Victor. In Jesus' name. Amen.

Intimacy
Passion
Vision
Evangelism
Multiplication
Family
Stewardship
Integrity

Discussion Guide

1. Start the session with an opening prayer.

2. Warm-up Question: Have you ever had a time in your life, either as a child or an adult, when you wanted to run away? Why?

3. Read the Core Value aloud at the beginning and end of the session together as a group.

4. After the group reads the Core Value, take a moment to discuss the following: Did it surprise you after becoming a Christian that life still has problems? Maybe even more problems? How did that make you feel?

5. In the shaded arrows labeled "Personal, External, Spiritual," have someone read the scriptures listed under each obstacle.

6. In the section titled "How Do You View Yourself?" discuss how your former life can hinder you from seeing yourself as God sees you.

7. In the section titled "Steps to Resolve Conflict," discuss the most common solutions for your family, work, and church environment. (Solutions: Lose-Lose, Win-Lose, Win-Win)

8. In the section titled "Biblical Perspective — You Are Provided the Armour of God," read Ephesians 6:10-18 aloud. Note the side bar quote, "If it has blood, it is not your enemy." Discuss how this applies to the Scripture.

9. Read the "Application — Living Christian to the Core" section, and as a group share and discuss strategies for overcoming obstacles.

10. End the session with a closing prayer.

Intimacy
Passion
Vision
Evangelism
Multiplication
Family
Stewardship
Integrity

Relevant Evangelism

The Power of Your Story

Core Value	God looks for men and women who live and share the Good News of Jesus Christ with cultural relevance, sensitivity, and power so that the eternal truth of the Gospel will be understood and received in every culture of the world.

Jesus gathers his closest followers for one more special meeting. He will deliver one of his most important messages. He will explain his purpose and give the disciples clear instructions.

Only a few days before, he had been brutally tortured and executed like a criminal. In his ordeal, Jesus revealed the hypocrisy of the priests, Pharisees, and other religious manipulators. He stood up to Pilate, who was Caesar's governor, manifesting an authority that far surpassed the power of Rome. Finally, he conquered death itself. Buried in a tomb on Friday evening, he was resurrected from the dead by the power of God on Sunday morning!

In this last gathering, Jesus speaks powerful words to his friends in an imperative tone. With the following statement, Jesus gives them a charge, a task, and a commission:

> *Then Jesus came to them and said, "All authority in heaven and on earth has been given to me. Therefore go and make disciples of all nations, baptising them in the name of the Father and of the Son and of the Holy Spirit, and teaching them to obey everything I have commanded you. And surely I am with you always, to the very end of the age." — Matthew 28:18-20*

This passage is known in Christianity as the Great Commission. It was intended for all of us who follow Jesus today. He commissioned us to carry out the grand task of revealing his Father's glory to the lost and hurting people around the world. He added that this mission would be possible through the power of the Holy Spirit. He gave his promise that he would be with us always (in Spirit when not in body).

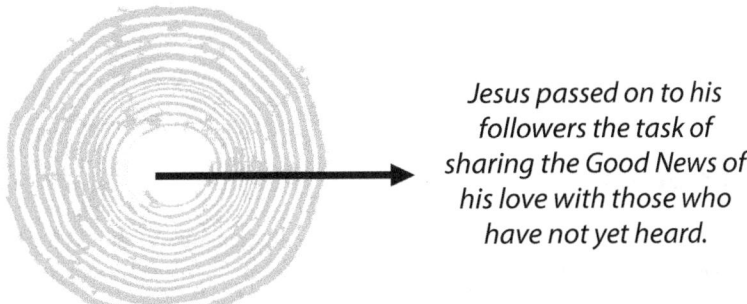

Jesus passed on to his followers the task of sharing the Good News of his love with those who have not yet heard.

Evangelism is Sharing the Good News

One of the terms used most frequently in the New Testament to describe the Christian message is the Greek word "euangelion," which means "good news." The English word "evangelism" is derived from that word and simply means "sharing the good news."

Intimacy
Passion
Vision
Evangelism
Multiplication
Family
Stewardship
Integrity

The Lausanne Committee on World Evangelisation defines evangelisation as:

> *The proclamation of the historical, Biblical Christ as Saviour and LORD, with a view to persuading people to come to him personally and so be reconciled to God.*

Read Paul's description in 1 Corinthians 9:19-23, and then explain this Scripture in your own words.

Describe what relevant evangelism means to you.

Going Deeper: For further study, read about Jesus' amazing sensitivity in John 4:1-42.

How to Share the Good News

The message of the Gospel is unique and cannot be compromised, but the methods of evangelism are diverse. Examples used today include mass media, public preaching, services to people in need, small groups, personal evangelism, and more.

What methods were instrumental in you becoming a follower of Christ?

The Power of Your Story

One of the most effective ways to share the Good News of Jesus Christ is on a person-to-person basis. Most people come to know Jesus Christ because of a friendship with a believer whose life example and personal testimony witness to God's love.

The New Testament records more than 35 examples of Jesus sharing the Good News with individuals in various circumstances, including when he was in severe pain on the cross. The essence of the Gospel is the life of a person, Jesus. Nothing communicates the truth of the Gospel better than a life transformed by the power of God. In 1 Peter 3:15, the apostle Peter writes that every Christian should be prepared to share his or her personal testimony in order to *"give an answer to everyone who asks you to give the reason for the hope that you have."*

Intimacy
Passion
Vision
Evangelism
Multiplication
Family
Stewardship
Integrity

How to Share Your Story

Your personal testimony should contain some element that helps another person understand how Christ can change his or her life. A model outline would include the following four points:

Life without Christ	Give a brief description of your life before following Christ.
How you became a Christian	Share what prompted you to seek Christ and how you encountered him.
Life with Christ	Explain how your life differs today from your past life.
Invitation to follow Christ	Invite the person to become a follower of Jesus Christ.

...How beautiful are the feet of them that preach the Good News of the Gospel of peace.

— Romans 10:15

In sharing your story, make clear the benefits of following Christ. Give examples from your personal experience. What difference has Christ made in your life? How has he led you or encouraged you? How is your life now more meaningful, purposeful, or significant? Touch on what life was like before Christ. Emphasise how you came to follow Christ and the positive changes that you have experienced. Use common language that the listener will easily understand.

Take time to hear their story. Try to understand where they have been, and share aspects of your story that will build a bridge into their experiences. Identify with them, be vulnerable, and help them understand the positive difference that Jesus can make in their life. Areas of your life that you can develop into your testimony include:

Before	**After**
Guilt	Forgiveness
Strife	Peace
Jealousy	Love
Emptiness	Fulfillment
Fear of death	Peace about death
Depression	Hope
Rejection	Acceptance
Loneliness	Friendship
Selfishness	Concern for others
Pleasure lover	Satisfaction in God
Fear of spirits, witchcraft, charms	Freedom from these fears

Going Deeper: For further study, read about Paul sharing his story with a king in Acts 26.

Sharing your Story

Reflect on God's grace in your life, and develop an outline of your testimony using the headings listed on the following page. Write the outline in the space provided, using words that will help you remember the message you want to share with the story of your life. After developing an outline, share your story with at least one other person.

Intimacy
Passion
Vision
Evangelism
Multiplication
Family
Stewardship
Integrity

My life without Christ:

How I became a Christian:

My new life with Christ:

An invitation to follow Christ:

Intimacy
Passion
Vision
Evangelism
Multiplication
Family
Stewardship
Integrity

Application — Living Christian to the Core

Now that you have prepared your story, spend time thinking about the world in which you live. What is the culture of your community and how does that culture shape how people experience life and themselves? Is it urban and highly secularised? Is income high or low? Is there a strong sense of community or pervading isolation?

Think of the stories you have heard other people share about their lives. **What are some of their hopes and dreams? How is success measured? What does failure look like? How can your testimony speak to those concerns?**

A Personal Challenge

Pause for a moment, and ask God to give you an opportunity this week to share your faith with another person. As you go through the next seven days, look for that opportunity. You may discover that God will give you several.

☐ Yes, I will look for an opportunity to share my story with at least one other person this week.

Prayer

Almighty God, thank you for the power of the Good News of Jesus Christ in my life. Help me share the Gospel with cultural relevance, sensitivity, and power so others will follow you.

Intimacy
Passion
Vision
Evangelism
Multiplication
Family
Stewardship
Integrity

Discussion Guide

1. Start the session with an opening prayer.

2. Warm-up Question: What does the word "relevant" mean to you? Give an example of something that is relevant, specifically in relation to effective evangelism.

3. Read the Core Value aloud at the beginning and end of the session together as a group.

4. Discuss what methods of evangelism were instrumental in your conversion.

5. Depending on the time, share your "story" in three minutes or less. At each future meeting, ask at least one person to share his or her "story."

6. End the session with a closing prayer.

Intimacy
Passion
Vision
Evangelism
Multiplication
Family
Stewardship
Integrity

46

Multiplication of Disciples
Fulfilling the Great Commission to "Go and Make Disciples"

Core Value	God looks for men and women who disciple, coach, and mentor others, who in turn become effective disciple-makers.

A farmer plants a seed in the ground, expecting it to grow into a fully mature plant that will produce fruit and develop seeds for other plants.

When you became a follower of Christ, God sowed a seed of godliness and abundant life in your heart; however, godly character does not happen randomly. It is developed over time through intentional effort as you inwardly come to know Christ and outwardly live in love and obedience to him.

With spiritual growth comes the challenge to multiply yourself in others, sharing what God is doing in your life and helping others grow to maturity in Christ. We are commanded by Jesus to "go and make disciples" so others can grow in their relationship with Jesus.

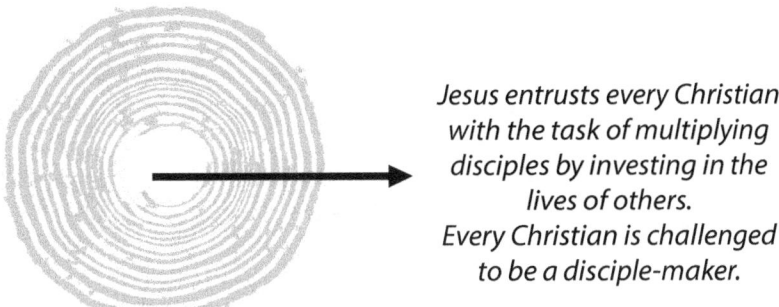

Jesus entrusts every Christian with the task of multiplying disciples by investing in the lives of others. Every Christian is challenged to be a disciple-maker.

The multiplication of disciples and development of leaders for the Kingdom of God involve discipleship, coaching, and mentoring. This session will focus on making disciples.

Discipleship – Grounding in the foundational principles of the Christian life.
Coaching – Imparting skills through a relational process from a more experienced Christian.
Mentoring – Being available so another person can achieve God's priorities for his or her life.

Definition of a Disciple and Discipleship

A **disciple** is someone who is living out the decision to follow Christ in everyday life. He or she is a person who knows Christ inwardly and is committed outwardly to living in love and obedience to him. **Discipleship** is the relational process of helping someone grow spiritually by:

Deepening the other individual's intimacy with God through prayer.
Building the principles of God's Word into that person's life.
Equipping him or her to understand and follow the promptings of the Holy Spirit.
Responding in obedience to any situation with Christ-like attitudes and actions.

Intimacy
Passion
Vision
Evangelism
Multiplication
Family
Stewardship
Integrity

When you became a Christian, did someone disciple you? If so, describe the process.

Jesus Christ: The Master Discipler

Jesus is the supreme example of how to make disciples. He selected key individuals and invested his life in them over a period of time. These men and women changed the course of human history by following his example. Jesus' secret is illustrated by a series of circles. The outermost circle in the illustration below represents his ministry to the world. The remaining circles can be followed to the core of his ministry and influence.

While Jesus had a large public ministry, his ministry of discipleship focused on investing in a few lives and helping them grow to spiritual maturity until they, too, were disciple-makers.

Circles of Influence

The Crowd — Large crowds followed Jesus. He preached and served by healing the sick and miraculously feeding thousands of people; however, the large crowds were not the main focus of Jesus' ministry. (Matthew 4:25, Luke 9:11)

CROWD

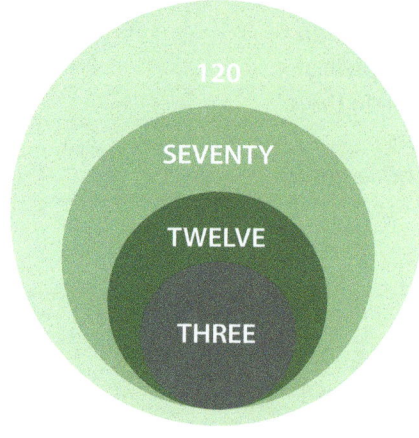

The One Hundred and Twenty — When the Holy Spirit came, there were one-hundred and twenty believers in Jerusalem. They were faithful followers of Jesus Christ. (Acts 1:15)

The Seventy — Jesus entrusted seventy disciples with a special task of travelling in groups of two to the villages where he was about to go preach. (Luke 10)

The Twelve Apostles — Jesus invested personally for three years in twelve of his followers; they are known as the Apostles. (Mark 3:14)

The Three — Jesus invested further in three of his closest disciples: Peter, James, and John. He took them when he raised the daughter of Jairus from the dead (Mark 5:37). They were present when Jesus was transfigured (Matthew 17:1-9), and Jesus met privately with them in the garden of Gethsemane the night before he was killed (Matthew 26:37). These three became the key leaders in the early Church.

Going Deeper: For further study, read 1 Peter 4. Reflect on what Jesus builds into Peter's life that Peter then passes on to us through his letter

Your life also involves a series of relationship circles. **Can you identify your different circles? Who is in your "crowd"? Who are your closest friends whom you can influence?**

Intimacy
Passion
Vision
Evangelism
Multiplication
Family
Stewardship
Integrity

Jesus' Command: Make Disciples

Jesus modeled disciple-making, and he gave a specific command to his followers in what is called the Great Commission. **Read Matthew 28:19-20, and then write the verses in the space below.**

Jesus arose very early, before sunrise and went to a lonely place to pray.

There are four verbs in the Great Commission. In the original Greek, the only imperative is to "make disciples" of all nations. The other verbs are the means by which we accomplish the task given by Jesus: going, baptising, and teaching.

Paul and Disciple-Making

Paul made disciples wherever he went. In his letter to a young man named Timothy, he encourages his disciple to multiply the principles of discipleship to others. **What instruction does Paul gives to Timothy in 2 Timothy 2:2?**

Paul expects Timothy to reproduce the discipleship process in others. In another New Testament passage, Paul writes to the Philippians with the following instructions:

> *Keep putting into practice all you learned from me and heard from me and saw me doing . . . — Philippians 4:9 NLT*

Discipleship is practical and focuses on real-life application. Paul's instruction to Timothy and the Philippians outlines a process of multiplication and guarantees the growth of the Church. You are a follower of Christ today because of this multiplication process that has been producing faithful disciples for almost 2,000 years.

This process began with Jesus and has continued to your generation.

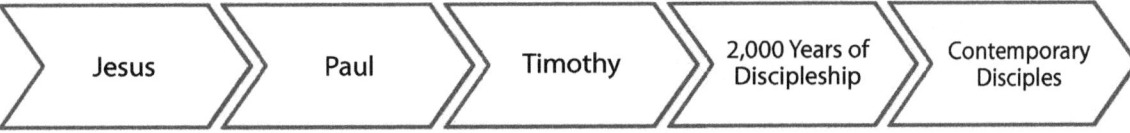

Jesus → Paul → Timothy → 2,000 Years of Discipleship → Contemporary Disciples

Going Deeper: For further study, read Acts 11:19-26 to discover the commitment to discipleship in the first generation of believers.

Intimacy
Passion
Vision
Evangelism
Multiplication
Family
Stewardship
Integrity

Take a few minutes to reflect on your life. **Who taught you the foundations of the Christian faith and helped you grow as a disciple of Jesus Christ? Write the name of the person or persons who discipled you in the space below. Share your story with at least one other person.**

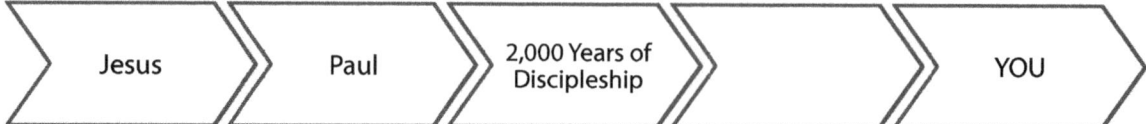

Jesus → Paul → 2,000 Years of Discipleship → → YOU

Characteristics of a Faithful Disciple

The following are four key characteristics of a faithful disciple. In the beginning of the discipleship process, these characteristics are seeds that need to be cultivated. As the disciple grows, these characteristics become more evident in his or her attitudes and actions.

Heart for God

A true disciple of Jesus will hunger for God's presence. They will look for opportunities to experience God and be in fellowship with him. David expressed his longing for God,

> As the deer pants for streams of water, so my soul pants for you, O God.
> — Psalm 42:1

Seekers and new followers of Christ often hunger for more of God in their lives. As understanding grows, their desire to continually experience God's presence and intimate fellowship in their lives only increases.

Available for God

God will bless and use those who are available to him. From the early stages, disciples need to open their hearts to God's voice. The prophet Isaiah exemplifies this characteristic when he describes his experience,

> Then I heard the voice of the LORD saying, "Whom shall I send? And who will go for Us?" And I said, "Here am I. Send me!" — Isaiah 6:8

Availability requires faith and a willingness to go where God sends. It may be tentative at first, but in time, the new disciple's faith will strengthen as he or she takes steps in the direction of God's purpose and will.

Faithful to God and Others

God is looking for those who will be faithful followers. Paul instructs Timothy to entrust the message to those who are reliable and faithful.

> And the things you have heard me say . . . entrust to reliable people who will also be faithful to teach others. — 2 Timothy 2:2

Faithfulness does not mean the disciple is absolutely perfect but that he or she is willing to let God lead his or her life. A faithful disciple desires to walk sincerely with God in the discipleship process.

Intimacy
Passion
Vision
Evangelism
Multiplication
Family
Stewardship
Integrity

Teachable Spirit

Invest in those who are willing to learn. In Matthew 13, Jesus compares those who hear God's teaching to different soils. The teachable person is compared to the fertile soil where the seed of God's Word grows and bears fruit.

> *But the one who received the seed that fell on good soil is the man who hears the word and understands it. He produces a crop, yielding a hundred, sixty or thirty times what was sown. — Matthew 13:23*

God is looking for these characteristics in your life and the lives of those whom you disciple. If these qualities are present and increasing, then a person will be growing toward spiritual maturity.

Which one of the characteristics of a faithful disciple listed above is your strongest? Which one do you need to strengthen?

Going Deeper: For further study, read Galatians 5 and discover the fruit of the Holy Spirit that results from discipleship.

Spiritual Disciplines — God's Path for Discipleship

Spiritual disciplines are tools that God uses in our lives to help us grow deeper in an intimate relationship with him. The word "discipline" is defined as "training that is expected to produce a specific character or pattern of behaviour."

Spiritual disciplines are a primary path that God uses to build godliness in our lives. There are many spiritual disciplines, including worship, meditation, fasting, and tithing. Three primary spiritual disciplines for a disciple are prayer, Scripture, and obedience.

A disciple is one who longs to follow Christ and grow in these areas. The clothes hanger is a good illustration of an intimate life with God and how these disciplines are essential for the development of a disciple. The disciple "hangs" on God through a relationship of intimacy. Then, just as all three sides of the hanger are essential for its usefulness, the three spiritual disciplines of prayer, Scripture, and obedience are essential in our lives. If a side is missing, the hanger will be off balance and will not be useful.

GOD

Intimacy

The Bible   Prayer

the disciple

Obedience

Prayer

Our depth of intimacy with God is directly related to the time we spend with him in the discipline of prayer. In Psalm 27, God tells us to seek his face. Prayer is growing deeper in our communication with him. You and those whom you disciple will be amazed at God's faithfulness as you pray. When meeting with those you disciple, always include significant time for prayer and covenant to pray over specific areas of your lives.

Intimacy
Passion
Vision
Evangelism
Multiplication
Family
Stewardship
Integrity

Scripture

Growing deeper in God's Word is the mark of a disciple. In his letter to Timothy, Paul advises his disciple with some important words of instruction. **What advice did Paul give to Timothy in 2 Timothy 2:15?**

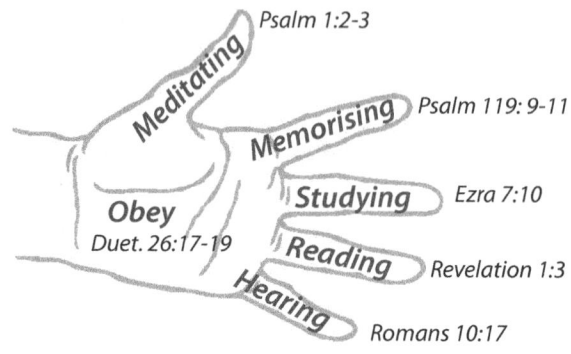

The human hand has five fingers. To properly grasp an object, every finger is required, and they all work together. The picture shows five specific disciplines you need to develop in order to properly handle the Word of God. God's Word is a key resource for understanding his purpose and plans. To help you remember this important discipline, draw your hand on a blank piece of paper and fill in the Scriptures. Read each passage and study it carefully.

Obedience

God's Word tells us that if we obey God's voice and Word, we will be blessed and anointed,

> *You have declared today that the LORD is your God. You have promised to obey his laws, commands, and regulations by walking in his ways and doing everything he tells you. The LORD has declared today that you are his people, his own special treasure, just as he promised, and that you must obey all his command. And if you do, he will make you greater than any other nation. Then you will receive praise, honour, and renown. You will be a nation that is holy to the LORD your God, just as he promised.* — Deuteronomy 26:17–19, NLT

Obedience is putting your faith to work in the your practical day-to-day life. Through obedience, your faith is proven; without practical obedience, your faith is dead (James 2:17).

Knowing that you set the example for a new believer, which of the above three qualities is your strongest and which one do you need to strengthen?

Going Deeper: For further study, read Acts 18:24-28, and identify the key qualities in the life of Apollos, a disciple taught by Paul's protege's Priscilla and Aquila.

Intimacy
Passion
Vision
Evangelism
Multiplication
Family
Stewardship
Integrity

Application — Living Christian to the Core

God looks for men and women who disciple others, who in turn become effective disciple-makers. Living Christian to the core means that you invest the time, prayer, and patience necessary to disciple others.

Spiritual reproduction is the goal.

Pray for clear direction from God as to whom you could disciple. Ask God to lead you to one or more people in whom you could make a life-to-life investment.

Reflect again on your discipleship timeline. **Rewrite the name or names of those who discipled you. Then, add the names of one or more whom you are discipling now or plan to disciple. What decisions do you need to make in order to make discipling others a higher priority in your life?**

It takes consistency and effort in your Christian life to inspire others to grow in their spiritual lives; yet, the result is one of the most satisfying experiences you will know as a follower of Christ. God will use you, and at the same time, you will become a deeper disciple who is faithfully fulfilling Jesus' words in the Great Commission to "go and make disciples."

The words of the Apostle John in his third letter powerfully express the joy of making disciples,

> *I have no greater joy than to know that my [spiritual] children are walking in truth.* — 3 John 1:4

The Prayer of the Disciple-Maker

> *Lord, lead me to the people whom I should disciple to be fully committed followers of you. Give me spiritual children, those in whom I will multiply myself through discipleship, who will walk in your truth and give glory to you. Amen.*

Intimacy
Passion
Vision
Evangelism
Multiplication
Family
Stewardship
Integrity

Discussion Guide

1. Start the session with an opening prayer.

2. Have someone share their "story" in three minutes or less.

3. Warm-up Question: If you have ever planted a garden or a tree, what kind of care and time did you give when it was first planted? Why?

4. Read the Core Value aloud at the beginning and end of the session together as a group.

5. In the section titled "Jesus' Command: Make Disciples" what do the scriptures tell us about our role in discipleship?

6. After reviewing the definitions of a disciple, share your experience of being discipled.

7. For an illustration, have someone bring two hangers to the group meeting. With one of the hangers, remove the hook. If there is no hook, does the hanger still work? The hook represents your intimacy with God, and without intimacy, your spiritual life will not work.

8. In the section titled "Characteristics of a Faithful Disciple," it is important to note: There are two distinct groups of people who need to be discipled. The first is a new believer who is hearing and learning about the basics for the first time. The newer generation comes from a broken society with little or no church-oriented background. More time may be needed to illustrate the new information. Then, there are "undiscipled disciples," or people who made a decision for Christ or even have been a part of a church for much of their lives, but they have never had anyone come alongside them with the basics. Their discussion will be more geared towards how they are now connecting the dots of what they knew in their mind but could not accomplish. As you look over the four basic characteristics of a faithful disciple (page 50), have them give their responses as to what their strengths are and what needs to be strengthened.

9. In section titled "Application — Living Christian to the Core" discuss what you need to add to your life in order for you to become a disciple-maker.

10. End the session with a closing prayer. As a group, read the Prayer of the Disciple-Maker.

Intimacy
Passion
Vision
Evangelism
Multiplication
Family
Stewardship
Integrity

Family Priority
God's Building Block for Society

Core Value	God looks for men and women who are convinced that the family is God's building block for society and give their family priority in their lives.

The family unit is the foundation for all cultures around the world. It constitutes the root of every nation. It is God's idea and design.

Family is where we first learn the skills of relating to others, where we learn to love and receive love, to listen, and to express our needs. God desires for the family to be a trusting and secure environment. In the family, we learn about authority, and hopefully, we learn healthy lessons about the consequences of disregarding that authority. God designed the family to be the place where babies are born and children are nurtured.

From Genesis to Malachi, and from Matthew to Revelation, God consistently uses family illustrations to describe his relationship with the human race. He also uses images from family life to characterise our shared relationships in the Church, the family of God. However, this unique institution is not without challenges.

Some people come from broken homes, filled with more pain than care. In Christ, the Father welcomes us into his family where lessons best learned at home may also be learned in the fellowship of the Church. Through the Church, we discover the freedom of true forgiveness; we find a community where we belong and a place where our gifts are welcomed. We also experience authentic affection through the Holy Spirit and our brothers and sisters in the Lord, who we often grow closer to than we thought possible.

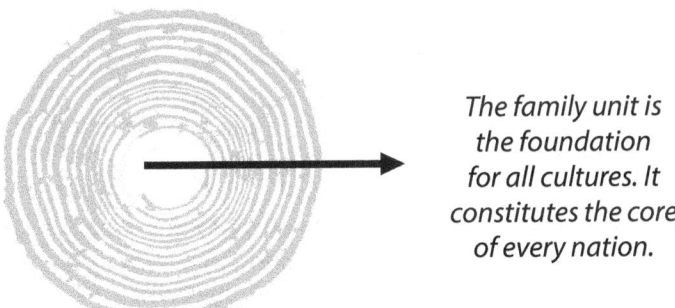

The family unit is the foundation for all cultures. It constitutes the core of every nation.

Negative forces threaten to weaken and destroy family structures in every human society. In modern societies, the divorce rate is high and growing, and these broken family relationships lead to troubled children. Unfortunately, Christians are not spared the effects of this changing scene in the lives of families. Christian homes are often places of blessing, but they can also be places of struggle and pain.

The Core Value of *Family Priority* strongly emphasises both the opportunities and challenges of the contemporary family. This Core Value calls us to be diligent about shaping the experiences in the lives of our family members.

Intimacy
Passion
Vision
Evangelism
Multiplication
Family
Stewardship
Integrity

The Family in Our Nation

While no single definition exists, the Bible clearly places great emphasis on the household in determining the legacy of one's family. **What is your definition of family? Who is in your family?**

What are some of the positive and negative forces impacting the family today?

How do those forces affect your family as you seek to live a faithful Christian life?

For this reason a man will leave his father and mother and be united to his wife, and they will become one flesh.

— Genesis 2:24

Going Deeper: For further study, examine the crises that confronted King David and his family in 2 Samuel 13-18.

Biblical Foundation — God's Perspective on the Family

Relationships are a central part of God's plan for his children. The truth is that we live in a time when "things" are often valued more than people. Children have become burdens rather than blessings. Many people sacrifice their families for opportunities of promotion or personal success. A text message is too often preferred over what is considered an inconvenient and time-consuming face-to-face conversation.

Now more than ever, Christians need to feel God's heartbeat for relationships. God intends for the family to teach the initial and essential skills of authentic community life. These vital skills and priorities are described in Matthew 22:36–40 and are called the Great Commandment. **Write out these skills below. How do they impact your life and relationships?**

Your first neighbour is your own family. In the Great Commandment, Jesus quotes Deuteronomy 6:5, which says to "Love the LORD your God with all your heart and with all your soul and with all your strength." Two verses later, Deuteronomy 6:7 says,

> *Impress [these commandments] on your children. Talk about them when you sit at home and when you walk along the road, when you lie down and when you get up.*

Intimacy
Passion
Vision
Evangelism
Multiplication
Family
Stewardship
Integrity

The Lord gives you a family so you can learn how to love him and others. As we grow in our ability to relate to those closest to us, we are able to take those skills into the broader community.

How do you see your family as a gift from God?

In what ways is your family a place to serve God?

What is your responsibility from God in your family?

Because God is love, he treasures relationships. His very nature is relational and he identifies himself in family terms: Father, Son, and Spirit.

*— Rick Warren
The Purpose Driven Life* [1]

Going Deeper: For further study, read about Joseph's care for his family, even after his brothers abandoned him, in Genesis 37-50.

God's Foundation for the Family

In the Bible, the building of a house often refers not to the dwelling in which the family lives, but to the family itself. Like a building, the family needs a strong foundation. If a building needs a foundation of stability and strength, the family needs a foundation of security and love.

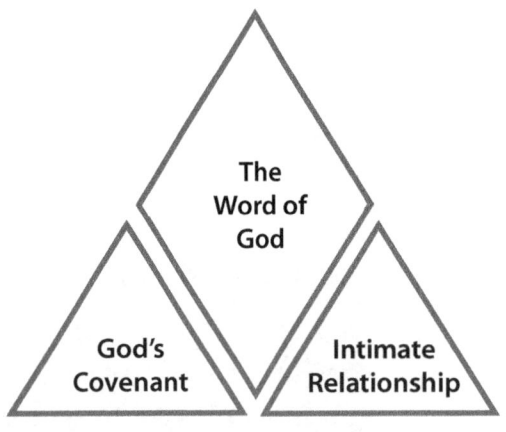

Of course, the best foundation for the family is the foundation of God himself. God provides the security and love upon which we build our families. God supplies us with three critical elements for the foundation of our homes. Further, Jesus compares the one who hears and practices his words to a man who built his house on the rock, and the storm could not destroy it.

The Word of God

The Bible shares the truth of who God is and what Christ has done before us. It tells us who we are and who God intends for us to be. When the Bible is at the heart of the family, the family dwells in security. **What are the two key elements in building a strong foundation as found in Matthew 7:24?**

Intimacy
Passion
Vision
Evangelism
Multiplication
Family
Stewardship
Integrity

God's Covenant

God's covenant is an unbreakable promise made that guarantees his own faithfulness. The covenant God made with Abraham served his family through the ages, and was passed on from generation to generation until the time of Christ and beyond. **What was God's promise to Abraham, found in Genesis 17:4, that applies to our generation?**

As believers, we share in the New Covenant provided for us in Christ. As participants in God's covenant, we anchor our family in the broader story of God and come to understand our place in God's work to reach the world.

Intimate Relationship

Through our intimate relationship with God, our families know that he is personal and real. They see how he relates to us and will come to desire to know him as well.

> We proclaim to you what we have seen and heard, so that you also may have fellowship with us. And our fellowship is with the Father and with his Son, Jesus Christ. — 1 John 1:3

As families, we participate in fellowship with the Lord and with his broader family, the Church.

Six Characteristics of Strong Families

| Strong Commitment |
| Spending Time Together |
| Good Communication |
| Appreciation and Affection |
| Ability to Solve Problems |
| Shared Spiritual Life |

Researchers in more than 30 countries have found remarkable similarities among families of different cultures. Families that describe themselves as strong commonly share a number of broad qualities or traits. In studying families around the world, it is significant to note that strong families in the global community are more similar to each other than they are different. The qualities they share in common far outstrip cultural distinctions. In short, God creates people for relationships, and we learn about relationships best within families in common ways. The researchers identified the following six important characteristics of strong families. [2]

Strong Commitment — Strong families believe in the value of the family and consider family a priority in their lives. They are dedicated to one another's well-being, and they invest time and energy in family activities. They recognise that sacrifices must be made for the sake of family togetherness, and family members make those sacrifices willingly.

Intimacy
Passion
Vision
Evangelism
Multiplication
Family
Stewardship
Integrity

58

Spending Enjoyable Time Together — Strong families spend time together doing meaningful things. One study of 1,500 school children asked, "What do you think makes a happy family?" Few children replied that money, cars, fancy homes, television sets, or trips to Disney World made a happy family. Most children thought of a happy family as one that is active together and that genuinely enjoys time spent with other family members.

Good Communication — Strong families communicate. In addition to commonplace exchanges, family members encourage one another to express their feelings and convictions, knowing that they will be received with respect and understanding.

Appreciation and Affection for Each Other — Strong families express appreciation for each other; they are intentional about encouragement and support. Family members seek to express their love in ways that others will receive as authentic. Families share a rich and genuine emotional life.

Ability to Solve Problems and React in Crisis — Strong families deal well with conflict. They have learned the value of using "win–win" strategies to solve disagreements. They face crisis situations with good communication and a sense of security. Family members are quick to be patient and readily forgive.

Shared Spiritual Life — Strong families have a shared spiritual life where, in the case of Christian families, the Bible, prayer, and worship are central. Such families experience faith as individuals and as a community. The family understands the importance of the spiritual well-being of each family member. This understanding is manifested in love, compassion, accountability, and celebration.

Build on Your Strengths

From the six characteristics of strong families, identify your strengths and weaknesses in the following three areas:

	Strongest	Weakest
1. Immediate Household	_____	_____
2. Extended Family Unit	_____	_____
3. Church Family	_____	_____

What elements, personalities, and practices contribute to your strengths?

These commandments that I give you today are to be upon your hearts. Impress them on your children. Talk about them when you sit at home and when you walk along the road, when you lie down and when you get up.

— Deuteronomy 6:6-7

Your first place of ministry begins across the breakfast table.

— Al VomSteeg ILI Senior International Director

Intimacy
Passion
Vision
Evangelism
Multiplication
Family
Stewardship
Integrity

Identify one characteristic from the list of family strengths that needs to be improved in your family. What can you do today to begin to work on that family characteristic?

Family — A Valuable Lesson

The most important lessons we learn in life are learned through our families, and the most important lessons that we teach in life are to our children. The lessons learned at home are taken with us into our communities and the world. Without question, the greatest gift we can give one another in our families is our love.

Additionally, in the fellowship of the family of God we find wise mentors through mothers and fathers in the Lord who can empower us to help our families. We discover the riches of God's Word that are filled with wisdom and empower us to create the kind of families that change the world through love.

Application — Living Christian to the Core

God looks for men and women who are convinced that the family is God's building block for society and give their family priority in their lives. Being Christian to the core means you recognise the most important relationships in your life are within your family, and the most important work that you will ever do is within your family.

God desires for you to be a blessing within your family. The following simple exercise can have a profound impact by helping you express this blessing.

On a separate document, write a blessing for a specific member of your family or to your family as a whole. In the blessing you might include:

- Expressions of affection.
- Affirmations of gifts, talents, and character traits.
- Thanksgiving for what this person means to you and your family, or what your entire family means to you.
- Your sense of God's dream for that individual or for your whole family.

After writing your blessing, find a way to share a copy with that family member or with your family as a group. By doing so, you may create a moment you and your family or family member will cherish for the rest of your lives. It is important to love those that God gives us to love.

Prayer

Dear God, your plan placed us in families. This act of grace reveals your wisdom. In families, we learn to love. Even though some families are broken, your perfect will is wholeness. You have provided for us grace, mercy, and forgiveness to restore and heal. For that which we have received from our families, we give you thanks. Help us by your grace to love our families as you have loved us. And as you give yourself for us, may we also give ourselves to our families so that they, too, may learn how to love. In Jesus' name, Amen.

Intimacy
Passion
Vision
Evangelism
Multiplication
Family
Stewardship
Integrity

60

Discussion Guide

1. Start the session with an opening prayer.

2. Have someone share their "story" in three minutes or less.

3. Warm-up Question: Name one family tradition you remember from your childhood or that you have started in your immediate family.

4. Read the Core Value aloud at the beginning and end of the session together as a group.

5. In the section titled "Biblical Foundation" have discussion on the family as a gift, a place of service, and a responsibility.

6. Discuss how common "God-talk" is in your home. Read Deuteronomy 6:7.

7. Discuss where your family is strongest among the six characteristics of a strong family. If you are comfortable doing so, share your family's weaknesses and a possible step you will take to strengthen a weak area. Keep this discussion brief.

8. This is one of the most inspiring and meaningful exercises in *Christian to the Core*. Read aloud the blessing you wrote for a family member.

9. Read the closing prayer aloud.

Intimacy
Passion
Vision
Evangelism
Multiplication
Family
Stewardship
Integrity

61

Faithful Stewardship
Effectively Managing Resources God Entrusts to You

Core Value	God looks for men and women who are faithful stewards of finances, time, and spiritual gifts in their personal lives and in their service to God and others.

Jesus taught his disciples the principle of stewardship by telling the story of a master and his three servants (Matthew 25:14–30). The servants were given different amounts of **money**, called "talents." The talent was a weight measurement in Jesus' time; one talent of silver or gold was equivalent to approximately 66 pounds. The master also gave a period of **time**—until his return—during which the servants were required to manage the talents. After some time, the master came back and called the servants to account for the money and time entrusted to them.

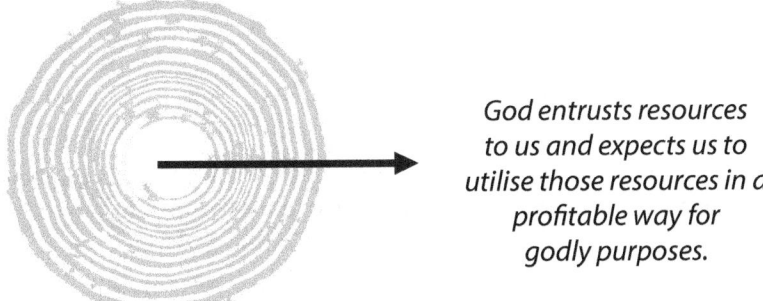

God entrusts resources to us and expects us to utilise those resources in a profitable way for godly purposes.

Your Money and Your Time

Reflect on your life and everything you own. **What are your most important material possessions? How were they acquired?**

Time is a valuable resource that God has given to each person. It is the most perishable resource because once it has passed, it is gone forever. Everyone is given the same amount of time each day. **Evaluate your effectiveness in managing time. Are you an excellent time manager, an average time manager, or a poor time manager?**

Intimacy
Passion
Vision
Evangelism
Multiplication
Family
Stewardship
Integrity

63

Biblical Foundation — Is it Really Mine?

Consider Psalm 89: 8-13:

> *O LORD God Almighty, who is like you? You are mighty, O LORD, and your faithfulness surrounds you. You rule over the surging sea; when its waves mount up, you still them… The heavens are yours, and yours also the earth; you founded the world and all that is in it. You created the north and the south.… Your arm is endued with power; your hand is strong, your right hand exalted.*

God's ownership is established by the fact that he created everything. The psalmist affirms God's power and authority — he controls the entire universe and the very forces of nature. The Bible clearly portrays God's right as owner of all things.

God is the creator of everything.	God is the owner of everything.	God is powerful and controls everything.
Psalm 24:1	*Deuteronomy 10:14* *Psalm 50:12*	*Romans 11:36* *Psalm 89:8-13*

Our Possessions

Consider the list of material possessions you identified on the previous page. **In light of Psalm 89 and the passages mentioned above, to whom do the things you possess really belong?**

Time is also a created entity. To whom does your time ultimately belong? Have you recognised the gift of time and given your time to God?

Going Deeper: For further study, consider Paul's sense of time management in Ephesians 5:11-20.

We Are Managers, Not Owners

In the very first chapter of the Bible, immediately after describing the creation of the human race, the Bible affirms that God created us to manage the earth's resources.

> *God blessed them and said to them, "Be fruitful and increase in number; fill the earth and subdue it. Rule over the fish of the sea and the birds of the air and over every living creature that moves on the ground."*
> *— Genesis 1:28*

Intimacy
Passion
Vision
Evangelism
Multiplication
Family
Stewardship
Integrity

God is the owner of all creation. Human beings are the administrators and stewards of God's creation. This includes our money, material properties, families, time, and even our bodies.

Managing Money

The Bible teaches three important stewardship principles that help us successfully manage the material resources that God entrusts to us:

I never would have been able to tithe the first million dollars I ever made if I had not tithed my first salary, which was $1.50 per week.

— John D. Rockefeller

1	**The Principle of Faithful Tithing** Leviticus 27:30 affirms that the tithe, which is ten percent of our income or the fruit of our labour, ". . . belongs to the LORD; it is holy to the LORD." Malachi 3:8-12 teaches the benefits of tithing. **What does God ask of us? What are God's promises to us?**
2	**The Principle of Sound Management** Tithing is the first step, but there is more to faithful stewardship. God owns the other 90 percent as well; our responsibility is to manage it wisely. God entrusts us and our wise management with the remaining 90 percent of resources. In Luke 14:28, Jesus uses the illustration of a man wanting to build a tower as he carefully considers the cost. We are responsible for effectively and efficiently managing resources with wisdom and purpose, according to balanced priorities.
3	**The Principle of Generous Giving** In Luke 6:38, Jesus says, "Give and it will be given to you. A good measure, pressed down, shaken together and running over, will be poured into your lap. For with the measure you use, it will be measured to you." Jesus promises to bless the generous. **How could this principle of "generous giving" affect other areas of your life to become "generous living?"**

Going Deeper: For further study, read 2 Corinthians 9:6-15.

Intimacy
Passion
Vision
Evangelism
Multiplication
Family
Stewardship
Integrity

Managing Time

The Bible teaches us to imitate Jesus. As in all other aspects of life, Jesus models wise time management. Examples from his life include:

1	**Jesus knew that his time was limited.** In John 9:4, Jesus makes this clear by saying, "As long as it is day, we must do the work of him who sent me. Night is coming, when no one can work."
2	**Jesus never lost sight of his purpose.** In John 17:4, Jesus prays, "[Father] I have brought you glory on earth by completing the work you gave me to do."
3	**Jesus understood that there is a right time to do the important things.** In John 4:35, Jesus says, "Do you not say, 'Four months more and then the harvest'? I tell you, open your eyes and look at the fields! They are ripe for harvest."

Reflecting on Jesus' use of time, select the greatest "time robber" in your life.

_____ Procrastination. "The greatest time wasted is getting started."

_____ Poor planning and scheduling.

_____ Lack of clear priorities.

The Blessing of Faithfulness

In the parable of the talents in Matthew 25:14-30, when the owner of the talents returned from travelling, he called each of his servants, the stewards, to give an account of what they had done with the resources that had been entrusted to them. The master praised those who had invested wisely and gave them more responsibility.

On another occasion, Jesus said, "Whoever can be trusted with very little can also be trusted with much" (Luke 16:10). God will entrust more resources to people who show themselves faithful with few resources. We are accountable to God for the wise and effective use of both our material resources and the time we are given on this earth. The simple awareness of this accountability should move us to rethink the use of these resources in our daily lives.

The Power of Positive Accountability

Imagine that God showed up today and asked you to give an account of your stewardship during the last month. **What would you report to God about your use of his money?**

Identify one thing you need to do differently in relation to material resources during the next month.

What would you tell God about the use of the 24 hours you have each day?

Intimacy
Passion
Vision
Evangelism
Multiplication
Family
Stewardship
Integrity

Application — Living Christian to the Core

God looks for men and women who are faithful stewards of material possessions and time in their personal lives and in their service to God and others. Effective stewardship is learned. Now that you are aware of what the Bible has to say on the subject, it is time to plan concrete steps to be faithful stewards of the resources God has entrusted into your hands. This session stressed important and practical principles for the management of two of the most important resources God has entrusted to you: time and money.

This Biblical teaching has immediate implications for the way we live and requires an observable response from us. You are invited to make a covenant with God through prayer and signing below. If God is the owner, then this is an opportunity for you to affirm your belief in that truth in a tangible way, recognising God as the source of your material resources and time.

As a good steward, commit to manage your resources according to God's purposes and priorities. And finally, live in such a way that you are always ready to give a good account of how you managed that which God entrusted to you.

Stewardship Covenant Prayer

LORD, I recognise that you are the owner of all that I have. I am only the administrator of the material resources that you have entrusted to me and the time I have to live. I commit to managing your resources wisely and ask your guidance to do so. Teach me to be a better steward of what I have, so I can be entrusted with more. In Jesus' name, Amen.

Today, I have sincerely prayed this prayer and made a stewardship covenant with God to faithfully manage his resources.

_____ , _____ , _____
Day   Month   Year

_____
Signature

Intimacy
Passion
Vision
Evangelism
Multiplication
Family
Stewardship
Integrity

68

Discussion Guide

1. Organise your time to complete the Stewardship Covenant at the end of the evening.

2. Start the session with an opening prayer.

3. Have someone share their "story" in three minutes or less.

4. Warm-up Question: (Allow 5-10 minutes for one or both of these questions.)

    *   If you won the lottery, how would you spend the money?
    *   Do you remember what you did yesterday between 10am -12pm? You actions, tasks, conversations, and even thoughts in the past are gone forever.

5. Read the Core Value aloud at the beginning and end of the session together as a group.

6. Read Matthew 25:14-30. Who does the Master represent? (. . .the journey, the talents, the servants). Was the Master fair?

7. In the section titled "Is It Really Mine?" discuss the difference between "mine" and "God's".

8. In the section titled "Managing Money," does there appear to be any connection between all three principles?

9. In the section titled "Managing Time," discuss Jesus' model of time management. Which of the "robbers" would be removed first in your life?

10. Read "Application — Living Christian to the Core," then pray the Stewardship Covenant Prayer together as a group.

11. If there is enough time, share what you have decided.

12. Before closing, draw attention to the website referenced in Session Ten (Page 73) for the spiritual gifts inventory. Complete the questionnaire prior to your next gathering. Please note that the web address is case sensitive.

13. End the session with a closing prayer.

Intimacy
Passion
Vision
Evangelism
Multiplication
Family
Stewardship
Integrity

The Gifts of the Holy Spirit
Your Spiritual Toolbox

Core Value	God looks for men and women who are faithful stewards of finances, time, and spiritual gifts in their personal lives and service to God and others.

Attempting to accomplish a task without proper tools can be frustrating and is often a recipe for failure. When God gives a vision and calls us to accomplish a task, he also freely provides the tools to accomplish that task. These tools include natural talents and abilities, as well as specific spiritual gifts, all of which are given to us by God. The most common Greek word used for spiritual gifts in the New Testament is "charisma." Broken down, this word is defined as:

"Charis" translates to "Grace"
"Ma" translates to "Result of"

Spiritual gifts result from God's grace. Like salvation, spiritual gifts are freely given from God to enable us to live the Christian life. The challenge is for Christians to discover, develop, and deploy spiritual gifts in order to effectively serve God and minister to people, with the result that the Kingdom of God comes on earth.

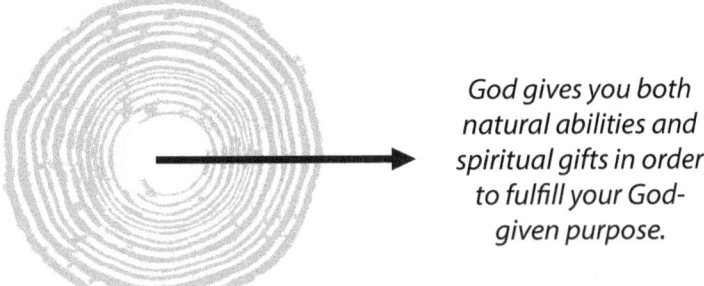

God gives you both natural abilities and spiritual gifts in order to fulfill your God-given purpose.

Biblical Foundations

Spiritual gifts are divine, supernatural abilities given by God that enable Christians to serve and minister to others. These special attributes are given by the Holy Spirit to every member of the Body of Christ, according to God's grace, for use within the context of the Body.

Four primary New Testament passages describe spiritual gifts. **Read the following Scriptures and make a list of the gifts mentioned in each:**

1 Corinthians 12:1-11 *The most extensive teaching on spiritual gifts in the New Testament.*

Intimacy
Passion
Vision
Evangelism
Multiplication
Family
Stewardship
Integrity

Romans 12:6-8 *An exhortation to use spiritual gifts according to the grace God gives.*

1 Peter 4:8-11 *A command to be good stewards of the gifts that God gives.*

Ephesians 4:11

> *So Christ himself gave the apostles, the prophets, the evangelists, the pastors and teachers, to equip his people for works of service, so that the body of Christ may be built up.* — Ephesians 4:11-12

List the offices of ministry that equip saints for the work of service.

Can you identify with any of the gifts or functions mentioned in these Scriptures? Which ones and why?

Welcome to the "Body"

Every Christian's vision is fulfilled in the context of the Church (capital "C" – the community of Christ-followers). One image that the Bible uses to describe the Church is the human body. The apostle Paul uses this image when he introduces spiritual gifts to the church in Rome.

> *Just as each of us has one body with many members, and these members do not all have the same function, so in Christ we who are many form one body, and each member belongs to all the others. We have different gifts, according to the grace given us.* — Romans 12:46

The image of the Church as a body is compelling because it has serious practical implications. Below are three key lessons from this Biblical truth that shape our daily lives as Christians in community.

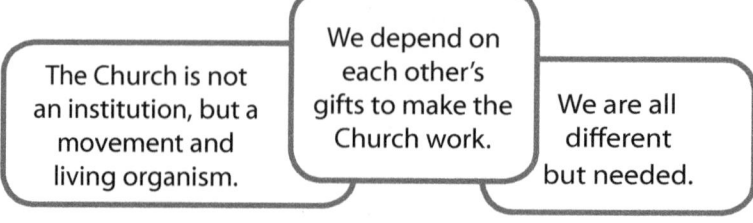

The Church is not an institution, but a movement and living organism.

We depend on each other's gifts to make the Church work.

We are all different but needed.

Intimacy
Passion
Vision
Evangelism
Multiplication
Family
Stewardship
Integrity

72

Of these three lessons, which is the most encouraging? Which is the most challenging?

Going Deeper: For further study, read Ephesians 3 and 4.

The Three Steps of Spiritual Gifts

1. Discover Your Gifts

You have unique spiritual gifts. Knowing those gifts will deepen your intimacy with God and empower you to serve others while fulfilling your God-given vision. Four primary methods help you discover your gifts:

Study	**Study** Biblical teaching on spiritual gifts.
Complete	**Complete** spiritual gift profiles and other resources. While not infallible, these can help guide your discernment.
	Visit www.BuildingChurch.net/g2s (case sensitive) to take a free online spiritual gifts inventory. This excellent resource takes only a few minutes to complete and will provide you with immediate feedback.
	An additional online survey that focuses on the nine task, or serving, gifts can be found in the Appendix on Spiritual Gifts.
Examine	**Examine** your life to discover the gifts you already use. As you grow in your understanding, you will recognise some gifts easily; others may surprise you.
Listen	**Listen** to mature members of the Body of Christ who can point you toward your gifts.

The Spiritual Gifts – Tools in Your Toolbox

Spiritual gifts are like tools you use to achieve your goals and vision in the Church. To better understand these tools and how to use them, you need to know the gifts that are available and how they work.

Gifts often come in clusters. If you have one particular gift, you may also have other gifts in that cluster. The 25 spiritual gifts that are listed in the New Testament are grouped below according to common clusters. You will have some degree of ability in many of the gifts listed below. Seek to identify your dominant gifts. (Find spiritual gift definitions in the Appendix.)

Communication Gifts – communicating with individuals or groups

Exhortation	Prophecy
Teaching	Evangelism

Every good and perfect gift is from above, coming down from the Father of the heavenly lights...

— James 1:17

Intimacy
Passion
Vision
Evangelism
Multiplication
Family
Stewardship
Integrity

Leadership Gifts – skills within the context of leadership

Administration	Leadership
Apostle	Shepherd
Missionary	

Practical Gifts – serving and helping others

Giving	Mercy
Help	Service
Hospitality	Voluntary Poverty

Sign Gifts – extraordinary or dramatic gifts that demonstrate the power of God

Deliverance	Tongues
Healing	Interpretation of Tongues
Miracles	

Resourcing Gifts – resourcing other gifts in furthering the Kingdom

Discerning of Spirits	Knowledge
Faith	Wisdom
Intercession	

No single passage of Scripture provides an exhaustive list of all the gifts. All gifts are important and are determined by a person's complete dependence upon the work of the Holy Spirit. Reflect on God's vision for your life. **How might spiritual gifts serve to achieve your vision? What evidence of these gifts do you see in your life?**

Gifts, Talents, and Roles

Spiritual gifts differ from natural talents because they involve the Spirit of God, but the two often accompany each other. A talent becomes a spiritual gift when deployed in the power of the Holy Spirit. Spiritual gifts are also different from Christian roles. All Christians perform different roles, even if they are not gifted in a particular area.

Hospitality	All Christians should show hospitality to others, but some have a gift in this area.
Giving	All Christians are expected to give tithes and offerings, but some have a gift in this area.
Evangelism	All Christians will witness to those who do not yet know Christ, but some have a gift in this area.

Going Deeper: For further study, read about the ministry of Barnabas, the "son of encouragement," in Acts 4:32-37, 9:26-30, and 11:19-30.

Intimacy
Passion
Vision
Evangelism
Multiplication
Family
Stewardship
Integrity

74

2. Develop Your Gifts

A faithful believer will work to develop his or her spiritual gifts. In 1 Timothy 4:14, Paul writes to Timothy, urging him to "not neglect your gift." In 2 Timothy 1:6, Paul again presses Timothy to

Fan into flame the gift of God, which is in you...

Every believer should discern his or her gifts and grow in the ability to use those gifts through greater knowledge and practical experience. Great Bible teachers do not become experts at using their gifts overnight. It takes a continual commitment to develop your gifts in order to deploy them most effectively.

Piano Playing – An Illustration of How to Develop Gifts

Almost anyone can learn to play the piano to some degree. Some people even have natural musical ability. However, without hard work and training, a pianist will never achieve his or her full potential.

The same holds true for spiritual gifts. Every believer has some ability for serving in many areas of the Body of Christ. However, God will give spiritual gifts to individual believers for them to serve more effectively. Those who grow in Christ develop their spiritual gifts to achieve their full potential and make the greatest possible impact for the Kingdom.

How are you developing your gifts to serve God and others?

3. Deploy Your Gifts

Your God-given spiritual gifts are intended to bring the Kingdom of God on earth in the power of the Holy Spirit. Scripture gives clear principles for deploying our spiritual gifts.

Seek Opportunities

> *So I was afraid and went out and hid your talent in the ground...*
> — Matthew 25:25

> *Anyone, then, who knows the good he ought to do and doesn't do it,*
> *sins.* — James 4:17

Faithful stewards seek opportunities to use their gifts. You can choose to use your gifts or not. Be a faithful steward of the gifts that God gives you, and look for opportunities to use them.

Intimacy
Passion
Vision
Evangelism
Multiplication
Family
Stewardship
Integrity

Exercise Your Gifts in Love

> *If I have the gift of prophecy… but have not love, I am nothing.*
> — *1 Corinthians 13:2*

Spiritual gifts enable us to serve; therefore, our motivation for using them should always be love. Without love, the apostle Paul says our gifts are worthless.

Anointed by the Spirit

> *…Apart from me you can do nothing. — John 15:5*

> *Then Peter, filled with the Holy Spirit, said to them… — Acts 4:8*

Spiritual gifts require the anointing and power of the Holy Spirit to function properly. In John 15, Jesus uses the illustration of a vine and branches to illustrate how we bear fruit by remaining connected to God.

Make a Difference This Week

Think of specific ways that you can use your spiritual gifts in the next seven days to advance the Kingdom of God on earth and make a difference in another person's life.

Share what you will do.

Intimacy
Passion
Vision
Evangelism
Multiplication
Family
Stewardship
Integrity

76

Application — Living Christian to the Core

God looks for men and women who are faithful stewards of the spiritual gifts that he entrusts to them. Spiritual gifts are tools in your "spiritual toolbox" that help you live Christian to the core. Every believer needs to discover, develop, and deploy their spiritual gifts in order to reach his or her full potential in the Body of Christ.

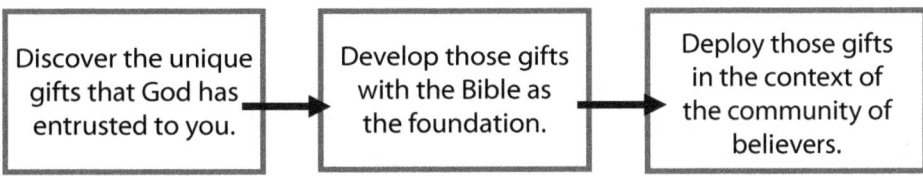

| Discover the unique gifts that God has entrusted to you. | → | Develop those gifts with the Bible as the foundation. | → | Deploy those gifts in the context of the community of believers. |

Through the gifts of the Holy Spirit, you will discover your special place in the Body of Christ. God will use your life to help bring the Kingdom of God on earth.

Prayer

> LORD, help me to discover my unique spiritual gifts. Teach me how to develop my specific gifts so I can use them effectively. Give me opportunities to deploy them for the good of the Church and for your glory. In Jesus' name, Amen.

Intimacy
Passion
Vision
Evangelism
Multiplication
Family
Stewardship
Integrity

Discussion Guide

1. Start the session with an opening prayer.

2. Have someone share their "story" in three minutes or less.

3. Warm-up Question: Which tools do you have in your toolbox at home? Why do you have more than one type of tool? How do you decide which tool to use? Read the opening paragraph to connect with the "toolbox of spiritual gifts."

4. Read the Core Value aloud at the beginning and end of the session together as a group.

5. Look at the difference between Spiritual Gifts and the Fruit of the Spirit (found in Galatians 5:22-23). Gifts are God-given and equip us to fulfill our vision. The Fruits of the Spirit are the result of our relationship with Christ.

6. In the section titled "Biblical Foundations," are any of the gifts listed with your name on them?

7. Take time to go around the group and affirm what strengths or gifts are seen in each other.

8. In the section titled "Gifts, Talents, and Roles," it is important to recognise the difference between "role" and a "spiritual gift".

9. Share the results of your online spiritual gifts inventory. The group will enjoy sharing their results and discussing with other group members. If someone has not yet completed an online profile, encourage them to do so.

10. You may see an immediate opportunity within your local church to use your gift(s). Consider asking your church leaders for a list of volunteer opportunities in the church and community. Share those opportunities with the group and invite others to use their spiritual gifts.

11. End the session with a closing prayer.

Intimacy
Passion
Vision
Evangelism
Multiplication
Family
Stewardship
Integrity

Integrity
Running the Race of Life and Finishing Well

Core Value	God looks for men and women of integrity who live holy lives that are accountable to God and to the Body of Christ. Integrity glorifies God, protects us from stumbling, and encourages growth.

John Stephen Akhwari is an Olympic legend. Representing his country, Tanzania, he was a favourite to win the marathon at the 1968 Olympics in Mexico City.

Well-rested. Ready. His expectations were high.

The Olympic marathon began in the afternoon of October 20, 1968. John Stephen Akhwari immediately moved to the front of the pack. Four hours later, only a few thousand spectators remained in Olympic Stadium. The winner of the race, an Ethiopian, had crossed the finish line more than an hour before, and the three medalists had already received their prizes in the last medal ceremony of the games.

As the lingering spectators prepared to leave, sounds of police sirens drew their attention to the stadium entrance. The gate opened, and the crowd began to cheer. John Stephen Akhwari was finishing the race. Earlier in the race he had fallen, slicing open his knee and dislocating the joint. Though officials urged him to quit and seek treatment, he refused. Bloodied and bandaged, he continued on.

Shaking and grimacing, he hobbled around the stadium track and finished the race. In that marathon, 17 of the 74 competitors did not complete the 26-mile race. Akhwari was not one of them. When asked why he continued in spite of his injury, knowing he had no hope of winning, the runner replied,

My country did not send me 5,000 miles to start the race;
they sent me 5,000 miles to finish it.

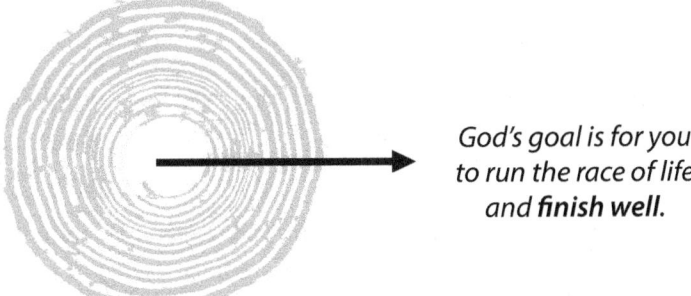

God's goal is for you
to run the race of life
*and **finish well**.*

Before you were born, God planned a life for you to be filled with his fullness and focused on a purpose to bring him glory. When you made the decision to follow Christ, you began a new life with a starting point and a finish line. Like John Stephen Akhwari, your goal is not merely to start, but to finish. God gives us the privilege of running the race set before us with ever increasing joy, faith, and obedience, not for ourselves, but for God who calls us. We can finish well and endure any hardship when we keep our eyes on Jesus. Many others have gone before us and finished well. **So can you.**

Intimacy
Passion
Vision
Evangelism
Multiplication
Family
Stewardship
Integrity

79

Have you ever felt like giving up in the midst of something significant? What did that experience feel like?

Biblical Foundation — Running the Race with Perseverance

Therefore, since we are surrounded by such a great cloud of witnesses, let us throw off everything that hinders and the sin that so easily entangles, and let us run with perseverance the race marked out for us. Let us fix our eyes on Jesus, the author and perfecter of our faith, who for the joy set before him endured the cross, scorning its shame, and sat down at the right hand of the throne of God. Consider him who endured such opposition from sinful men, so that you will not grow weary and lose heart. — Hebrews 12:1-3

When these words were written, the games of the ancient Olympiad still thrilled the Mediterranean world. Athletes prepared with dedication for the competition. Wars were halted to ensure safe travel. The victors were celebrated as heroes, and they were showered with wealth and honours.

The writer of Hebrews used the Olympic Games to call us to spend ourselves in preparation like these athletes, not for an olive wreath crown or worldly fame, but for the glory of Jesus who "endured the cross, scorning its shame."

Two basic elements enable us to finish well in "the race marked out for us." The first is to be a person of integrity, who is the same on the inside as on the outside. The second is to live in active fellowship, receiving the encouragement and accountability that we need from others who are in the same race and share the same goal of finishing well.

> *The content of your character is your choice. Day by day, what you do is who you become. Your integrity is your destiny.*
>
> *— Heraclitus of Ephesus, Greek Philosopher, c. 535–475 B.C.*

The Race Requires Integrity and Accountability

Integrity – The Great Challenge

Who may ascend the hill of the LORD? Who may stand in his holy place? He who has clean hands and a pure heart… — Psalm 24:3-4

The author of Psalms recognises that outward performance is inadequate without the inward reality of a "pure heart." The English word "hypocrite" comes from the Greek word for actor, "hypokrites," meaning "one who plays a part." A hypocrite is someone who hides his or her true self and cannot be trusted. Hypocrites are unpredictable for they lack commitment to anyone or anything outside of themselves. In simple words, they lack integrity.

In contrast, James 1:12 reflects that a person of integrity "perseveres under trial," "has stood the test," and "will receive the crown of life." Two critical aspects of integrity are the inward quality of the heart and the outward expression of that inward reality seen in our actions. A person of integrity is the same in heart, mind, and actions, regardless of circumstances. We can think of integrity in three dimensions:

Intimacy
Passion
Vision
Evangelism
Multiplication
Family
Stewardship
Integrity

Integrity is **What I Am: Whole**

Jesus models integrity by living an integrated life. His life was whole, not compartmentalised or confused with competing loyalties. His inner life of devotion to God and his outer life of action were consistent, and the crowds recognised it. **Why was Jesus called a man of integrity in Mark 12:14?**

Integrity is **What I Stand On: A Commitment to My Promises**

Integrity ensures reliability—to speak what is simply true, avoid exaggeration, and promise only what can be delivered. Jesus was faithful to the words he spoke and the promises he made, and he called his followers to the same simple standard. **Write out Jesus' simple standard found in Matthew 5:37.**

Integrity is **What I Do: Actions Consistent with My Beliefs**

Our actions reflect our beliefs. It is critical that our actions be consistent with God's command for integrity. To paraphrase St. Francis of Assisi, a person of integrity can preach, and if necessary, use words. **In Matthew 7:21, who does Jesus say will enter the Kingdom of heaven?**

What do you find to be the greatest challenges to maintaining integrity?

What individuals in your life are impacted the most by your integrity? How are they impacted?

Going Deeper: For further study, read Jesus' Sermon on the Mount in Matthew 5-7.

Intimacy
Passion
Vision
Evangelism
Multiplication
Family
Stewardship
Integrity

Accountability – Encouragement to Live a Life of Integrity

The second element that enables us to finish our race well is to live in active fellowship, receiving the encouragement and accountability we need from others who are in the same race and share the same goal. God is aware of your challenges and struggles as you seek to be a person of integrity. He knows you need help to "throw off everything that hinders and the sin that so easily entangles" (Hebrews 12:1).

J. B. Phillips translates Romans 12:2 in a wonderful way,

> *Don't let the world around you squeeze you into its own mold, but let God re-mold your minds from within, so that you may prove in practice that the plan of God for you is good, meets all his demands and moves toward the goal of true maturity.*

The "goal of true maturity" is to live a life of integrity. God wants to re-mold us to his standards. Accountability is the bridge that spans the gap between wanting to live with integrity and being a person of integrity. There are four levels of accountability:

Accountability to God

Our most intimate fellowship will always be with the Lord through his Spirit. He meets with us in the intimate and secret places of our hearts. For that reason, it is no surprise that Romans 14:12 says, "Each of us will give an account of himself to God." The God who made us also fills us with his love that we might be encouraged to press on to his highest standard.

Accountability to Ourselves

We can be our own worst critics, but as we respond to God's grace, he restores our conscience. He quiets the evil-speak of our self-talk and calls for our actions to be consistent with the truth. Paul writes to his associate, Timothy, "Watch your life and doctrine closely" (1 Timothy 4:16).

Accountability to an Intimate Few

The intimate few are our closest friends, the trusted few who know our story and share our dreams. Proverbs 27:17 says, "As iron sharpens iron, so one man sharpens another." These intimate few grow with us. We willingly submit ourselves to them, and we trust their advice because they have our best interests at heart.

Accountability to the Community of Faith

As Christians, we are part of a community of faith that is the Church, the Body of Christ (1 Corinthians 12:27). In the midst of this broader fellowship, we give and receive spiritual nurture and guidance. In the Church, God makes accountability possible through an environment of grace, a place to find wise men and women willing to give their counsel and encouragement (Acts 14:26-28).

How can you create an environment of grace and facilitate the practice of accountability in your life?

Intimacy
Passion
Vision
Evangelism
Multiplication
Family
Stewardship

Integrity

82

Who is your support system and why are they important?

Going Deeper: For further study, read about Paul's instructions to Timothy in 2 Timothy 2.

Finishing Well: Our Goal Is the Finish Line

John Stephen Akhwari finished well. His Olympic race had a start and a powerful finish. When you began your Christian life, you started the race with a purpose to bring glory to God and live a life of fullness. Akhwari prepared himself to do what was necessary to finish what he started. He did not have to be first; however, to be successful, he did have to cross the finish line.

You started *Christian to the Core* by exploring what it means to know God personally through the Core Value of *Intimacy with God*, your starting point. You kept a focus on God's vision for your life as you reflected upon the Eight Core Values. Each Core Value is important in helping you cross the finish line.

Paul lived his life as a faithful follower of Jesus Christ, from his dramatic conversion on the Damascus road, to his death as a martyr. He finished well. In his last letter, Paul wrote,

> *I have fought the good fight, I have finished the race, I have kept the faith. Now there is in store for me the crown of righteousness, which the Lord, the righteous judge, will award to me on that day.*
> — 2 Timothy 4:7-8

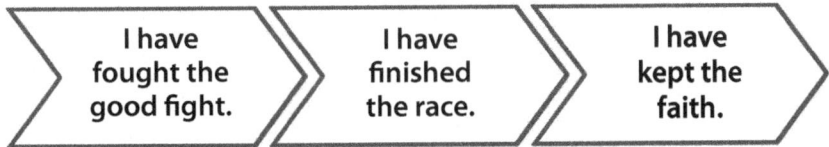

He Fought the Good Fight. Paul's life was not an easy life by any measure. He lived a faithful life, no matter what the cost.

He Completed the Race. Paul's goal was to finish well. Any difficulty he encountered only brought him closer to that goal.

He Kept the Faith and Finished Well. Nothing was more important to Paul than maintaining his intimate walk with the one who saved him. Beyond the finish line for Paul was the ultimate prize, "the crown of righteousness, which the Lord, the righteous judge, will award to me on that day — and not only to me, but also to all who have longed for his appearing" (2 Timothy 4:8).

Intimacy
Passion
Vision
Evangelism
Multiplication
Family
Stewardship
Integrity

Application — Living Christian to the Core

God looks for men and women of integrity who live holy lives that are accountable to God and to the Body of Christ. Integrity glorifies God, protects people from stumbling, and encourages growth.

After assessing his life, Paul writes that heaven is not only for him, "but also to all who have longed for his appearing." We are the "all" that Paul had in mind. He fought the good fight, he finished the race, and he kept the faith, not only for Christ's sake, but for ours. Your challenge to finish well is not only for yourself, but for the sake of those closest to you and for those who watch you to decide if they also should commit to this race.

Keep your focus. Run well. Finish the race.

Identify two or three people, of your same gender, who love God and also love you. Ask them to be your accountability partners. Their charge is to help watch over your life so you can finish well the race of life. Meet with them periodically, encourage one another, and pray together.

Like Paul, one day you will be able to say, "I fought the good fight. I finished the race. I kept the faith."

The Finisher's Prayer: Acts 20:24

> *Almighty God, I now pray the prayer of the finisher, which Paul spoke of in Acts 20:24. "However, I consider my life worth nothing to me, if only I may finish the race and complete the task the Lord Jesus has given me — the task of testifying to the Gospel of God's grace." Amen.*

Intimacy
Passion
Vision
Evangelism
Multiplication
Family
Stewardship

84

Integrity

Discussion Guide

1. Start the session with an opening prayer.

2. Have someone share their "story" in three minutes or less.

3. Read the Core Value aloud at the beginning and end of the session together as a group.

4. After the introduction story on the Olympic marathon, share a time when you wanted to give up.

5. In the section titled "Integrity — The Great Challenge," express the three components of integrity in your own words.

6. As a group, discuss how to encourage someone while also holding them accountable.

7. In the section titled "Finishing Well: Our Goal is the Finish Line," discuss the span of Paul's life and why "finishing the race" came before "keeping the faith"?

8. Read the "Application — Living Christian to the Core," and then as a group, pray the Finisher's Prayer as your commitment and closing prayer.

Intimacy
Passion
Vision
Evangelism
Multiplication
Family
Stewardship
Integrity

Living Christian to the Core
God is at Work in You

Living Christian to the core is an adventure in the Kingdom of God, and this twelve-session journey is a beginning point to live the rest of your life. The lure of the Eight Core Values will stimulate and challenge you for the rest of your life as the Holy Spirit makes you into the person God has called you to be. One person said, "Living by the Eight Core Values is better the second year than the first." Another person responded, "I have been living by the Eight Core Values for five years now. Each year is better than the previous year as I experience more and more of the presence and power of God in my life." The values are rooted in an amazing truth:

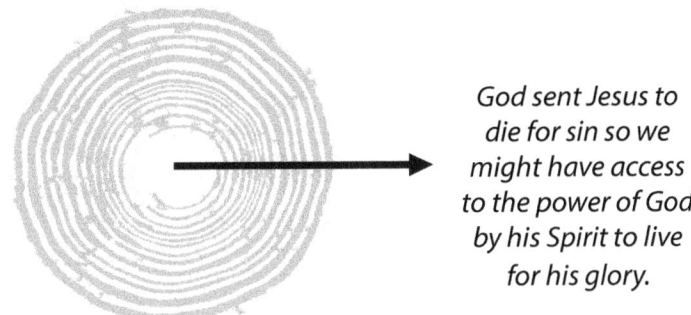

God sent Jesus to die for sin so we might have access to the power of God by his Spirit to live for his glory.

...Freely you have received, freely give.

— Jesus
Matthew 10:8

The Bible calls this amazing truth, salvation. It is God's gift to all who receive him through Jesus Christ. It is the passionate invitation that we extend to people throughout the world. We began this study with a powerful statement from the prophet Habakkuk,

> *Look at the nations and watch — and be utterly amazed. For I am going to do something in your days that you would not believe, even if you were told. — Habakkuk 1:5*

Around the world, God is moving to reveal the power and promise found in Jesus Christ. In Eastern Europe, young people are accepting the challenge to step up to a lifetime of Christian leadership. In Africa, signs and wonders continue to sweep across the continent, validating the proclamation that Jesus is Lord. Across the world of Islam, Muslims are experiencing dreams and visions where they see Jesus as he calls people to follow him.

In China, believers are responding to God's call to plant churches along the Silk Road and back to Jerusalem as part of the fulfillment of Joel 2. Across Latin America, God is moving powerfully as thousands of people turn to Christ every day. And in North America, while mainline denominations struggle, God is raising up new ministries and church planting movements to renew and re-evangelise America. Truly, God is working across the world, pouring his grace into the hearts of those who are seeking him.

Read John 4:1-30. **What did the woman of Samaria do when she realised who Jesus was? What was the result?**

Intimacy
Passion
Vision
Evangelism
Multiplication
Family
Stewardship
Integrity

Biblical Foundation — It is God Who Works in You

The key to unlocking the dynamism of the Eight Core Values is the intentional application of these Biblical practices in submission to the Holy Spirit.

> *Therefore, my dear friends, as you have always obeyed — not only in my presence, but now much more in my absence — continue to work out your salvation with fear and trembling, for it is God who works in you to will and to act according to his good purpose.*
> *— Philippians 2:12-13*

God is at work in us and through us. That is the conviction we share. This is God's plan. God pursues us constantly and relentlessly, working to reveal himself in a twisted world and broken lives. When we discover him, he pours himself into our brokenness. He teaches us who he is and how he works.

God met with Moses face-to-face as a man meets with a friend. God will meet with you because he is faithful. Continue to work out your salvation, for it is God who will complete the good work he has begun in you.

Stick to the Basics

You now know what it means to live Christian to the core; it is no longer a mystery. The challenge is to stay true to the basics, and to focus on the foundation. In his preface to the second edition of *A Long Obedience in the Same Direction*, Eugene Peterson writes,

> *God doesn't change: he seeks, and he saves. And our response to God as he reveals himself in Jesus doesn't change: we listen, and we follow. Or we don't. When we are dealing with the basics — God and our need for God — we are at bedrock.* [1]

We are dealing with the basics. There is no surprise that when we started working with Eight Core Values around world, the reception was exciting and grateful. In every culture, and in every language, when we introduced the Eight Core Values as essential practices of the Christian life, people responded with great enthusiasm. These individuals take what they have learned and immediately share it with others, and they report back with great passion that "God is at work!" They bear witness to a deep sense of God's intentionality; this is how God calls us to live in the world.

Tradition holds that St. Augustine said,

> *Without God, we cannot. Without us, he will not.*

God initiates his work by calling us to surrender our lives to him through Christ. As the Holy Spirit fills us, we begin to grow. As He moves in our understanding, we begin to order our lives around what He reveals in the Bible and the applied wisdom of Scripture in the Church.

Intimacy
Passion
Vision
Evangelism
Multiplication
Family
Stewardship
Integrity

The Eight Core Values invite a greater intentionality in conformity with God's revealed will. As you respond, the Holy Spirit increases his activity and power through your life. God reveals his grace, people come to Jesus, and God is glorified.

Being grounded in the basics and rooted in the fundamentals are vital to any successful effort. God is using faithful people around the world to reveal his glory. These individuals are not necessarily the smartest or most educated, and they are certainly not the richest or most powerful from the world's perspective. What sets these faithful, fruitful people apart is that they have done the simple but diligent work of anchoring their lives in the Eight Core Values of the most effective Christians. They are changing lives and glorifying God, and now you have joined their ranks.

Expectations Fulfilled

In the beginning we asked you to identify your expectations for this journey. Go back to the first page in this notebook, and review what you wrote. Spend time reflecting over your experience during these weeks.

What topics or Core Values have you learned more about?

What have you learned how to do?

How is your life different?

Intimacy
Passion
Vision
Evangelism
Multiplication
Family
Stewardship
Integrity

Going Deeper: For further study, read how Paul prays for the Church in Ephesus in Ephesians 1:15-23.

Reflecting on the Eight Core Values — What Have You Discovered?

We began this study with the Core Value of *Intimacy with God*. In the last session, we examined the Core Value of *Integrity*. The other six Core Values stand between these two great bookends.

If our intimacy is deep and our integrity uncompromising, the remaining values can also stand strong in our lives.

God is at work everywhere. He is at work in you. When you embrace the commitments implicit in the Eight Core Values, you invite the Lord to use you for his glory. Take the next few minutes to reflect upon the Eight Core Values and the role they can play in your life.

Intimacy with God is an eternal journey. The God of time and eternity invites us to know him more and more. We will never plumb the depths of his goodness, but he always draws us into greater revelations of his marvellous grace.

> **I have discovered that . . .**

Passion for the Harvest is the eternal flame that touches our hearts and fills us with love and purpose. It burns afresh with each new encounter of lost souls that have yet to experience the amazing love of God in Christ.

> **I have discovered that . . .**

A Visionary Life is a lifestyle of purpose that is uniquely crafted around your gifts and the needs of others. God's plan is to reveal his glory and to help bring the Kingdom of God on earth through you.

> **I have discovered that . . .**

Intimacy
Passion
Vision
Evangelism
Multiplication
Family
Stewardship
Integrity

Culturally Relevant Evangelism is sharing the Good News of Jesus Christ. You have a powerful story to share of God's grace in your life.

> **I have discovered that . . .**

Multiplication of Discipleship invites spiritual fruitfulness as God uses you to implant the very life of Christ in the hearts of others.

> **I have discovered that . . .**

Family Priority declares that family is the building block of all relationships and our first place of influence. As we continue to care for our family, we are more able to care far beyond that intimate circle.

> **I have discovered that . . .**

Faithful Stewardship actualises the blessings of Christ's Lordship over our lives and all creation. Through stewardship, we honour God and invite his blessings in our lives.

> **I have discovered that . . .**

Integrity is life lived according to design. A life of holiness before God and one another bears witness to the righteousness of God in a skeptical but hurting age.

> **I have discovered that . . .**

Intimacy
Passion
Vision
Evangelism
Multiplication
Family
Stewardship
Integrity

Of the Eight Core Values, which have impacted your life the greatest since this journey began? Why?

Of the Eight Core Values, which do you feel need to be strengthened the most in your life?

Identify two or three people who could help you grow in the areas you listed above. Ask them to help you go deeper in these specific areas.

You Are Different Now

John makes a remarkable statement in 1 John,

> *How great is the love of the Father has lavished on us, that we should be called the children of God! And that is what we are! The reason that the world does not know us is that it did not know him. Dear friends, now we are children of God, and what we will be has not yet been made known. But we know that when he appears, we shall be like him, for we shall see him as he is. — 1 John 3:1-2*

"We shall be like him." We shall love as he loves and with his passion for people. We shall forgive with his infinite capacity to release people from the wrongs and offences they commit against us. We shall look into hearts with compassion and a willingness to do something to make a difference. We shall rally others to the work of lifting high the name of Jesus, and they shall gather because they recognise the presence of the Holy Spirit in our surrendered hearts.

Paul echoes this expectation,

> *Now the Lord is the Spirit, and where the Spirit of the Lord is, there is freedom. And we, who with unveiled faces all reflect the Lord's glory, are being transformed into his likeness with ever-increasing glory, which comes from the Lord, who is the Spirit. — 2 Corinthians 3:17–18*

Intimacy
Passion
Vision
Evangelism
Multiplication
Family
Stewardship
Integrity

As you live the Eight Core Values, you become Christian to the core. The Holy Spirit's presence in our lives works relentlessly to transform us into people who reflect God's glory. As others experience our love and care, they want to know how it is possible for us to live the life we lead.

Countless individuals in the Church read about this type of fulfilled life in the Bible, and they hear it proclaimed from the pulpit. They truly desire to get there, but they do not know how.

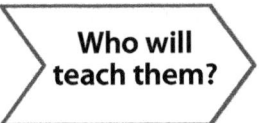

Still, many more outside of the Church long to live lives of purpose and love but are lost in endless gimmicks and promotions that promise everything, and deliver nothing.

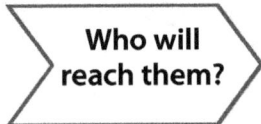

Who will teach them? Who will reach them?

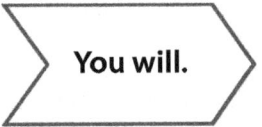

That has been Jesus' plan all along.

> Then Jesus came to them and said, "All authority in heaven and on earth has been given to me. Therefore go and make disciples of all nations, baptising them in the name of the Father and of the Son and of the Holy Spirit, and teaching them to obey everything I have commanded you. And surely I am with you always, to the very end of the age." — Matthew 28:18-20

The Eight Core Values are remarkable because they equip you to do what Jesus has called you to do. What you have yet to learn, Jesus will teach you – he is with us always! – as you live these basic, yet powerful values.

You are not alone. There is a mighty company of men and women around the world who are rallying to Jesus' call. Like you, they have been equipped for the work, empowered for the task, and are living for God's glory.

Intimacy
Passion
Vision
Evangelism
Multiplication
Family
Stewardship
Integrity

Application – Live for His Glory

God created you for a purpose, and the Eight Core Values are God's way of enabling you to fulfill that purpose. Now that you have completed this discipleship journey, you have the opportunity to serve others by sharing these values with them. Paul instructs Timothy,

> *And the things you have heard me say in the presence of many witnesses entrust to reliable people who will also be qualified to teach others. — 2 Timothy 2:2*

As you help others live Christian to the core, these values will become more deeply rooted in your own life, and you will discover the depths of the riches to be found in the Kingdom of God.

Using *Christian to the Core*, you can take others on the journey that you have experienced. You do not need special training. Your personal experience qualifies you to help others, although resources are available at ChristiantotheCore.org.

Don't delay. Will you take others on the journey?

God is looking for men and women who will invest the Eight Core Values in another person's life. If you will invest in another person, then your life will never be the same. In fact, it will be one of the most satisfying things you have ever done. And the lives of those you equip will never be the same.

Take a few minutes now to pray. Ask God to show you one or more people who you could contact this week to share what you have discovered. **Write their names below.** Let another person's journey begin soon!

Commitment Prayer

> *The Spirit of the Sovereign LORD is on me, because the LORD has anointed me to preach good news to the poor. He has sent me to bind up the brokenhearted, to proclaim freedom for the captives and release from darkness for the prisoners, to proclaim the year of the LORD's favour... they will be called oaks of righteousness, a planting of the LORD for the display of his splendour. — Isaiah 61:1-4*

Intimacy
Passion
Vision
Evangelism
Multiplication
Family
Stewardship
Integrity

Discussion Guide

It is time to celebrate!

1. In the Jewish tradition, in order for each generation to remember God's faithfulness on their journey to the Promised Land, they set aside special times to celebrate what God has done. Find a way to make this session a special celebration. Consider a special meal or refreshments.

2. Start the session with an opening prayer.

3. Warm-up Question: What events in your life have caused you to stop and celebrate?

4. Have two or three people share their "Expectations Fulfilled."

5. Review the Eight Core Values by inviting people to share what they have discovered. Give people time to express themselves, but keep moving forward.

6. Go around the group and invite people to share the Core Values that have had the greatest impact in their lives during the study. Then, invite participants to share areas where they need to grow the most and any action plans they have developed for going deeper.

7. Very important. Research shows that a person learns 95 percent of what he or she teaches someone else. You challenge is to take someone else through *Christian to the Core*. This could be done one-on-one or with a small group. It could be done with your children or grandchildren. Ask your group leader if he or she is available as a coach and mentor as you disciple someone else in the Eight Core Values.

    As a leader, this may be the most important action you take to help others live Christian to the core. The global ILI Team discovered that those who multiply their experience to others encounter more of the power and presence of God than those who do not equip others. Discipleship is a ministry of all believers.

    Take a step of faith. Make sure to register at <u>ChristiantotheCore.org</u> to receive updates, information, and devotional resources.

8. For your final prayer, use Isaiah 61:1-4. This was the text that Jesus used to announce his ministry. As a follower of Christ, you are to pray this prayer and depart to follow his example.

Amen!

Intimacy
Passion
Vision
Evangelism
Multiplication
Family
Stewardship
Integrity

Endnotes

Welcome

1. Proverbs 1:1-6, 11:28, 30; Jeremiah17:7-8; Isaiah 61:1-4; Luke 4:16-20
2. George Barna, *Maximum Faith*, (Venture, CA: Metaformation Inc., New York, NY: Strategenius Group LLC, Glendora, CA: WHC Publishing, 2011).

Session 2: Intimacy with God

1. Richard J. Foster, *Celebration of Discipline: The Path to Spiritual Growth*, 3rd ed. (New York: HarperCollins Publishers, 1988), 1.

Session 3: Passion for the Harvest

1. Wesley Duewel, *Ablaze for God* (Grand Rapids: Zondervan, 1989), 107.
2. Ibid., 108.
3. Billy Graham, *Calling Youth to Christ*, (Grand Rapids: Zondervan, 1947), 45.
4. Mother Teresa, Brian Kolodiejchuk (ed), *Mother Teresa: Come Be My Light — The Private Writings of the Saint of Calcutta* (Doubleday Religion, 2007), 416.
5. "U.S. Food Aid Reducing World Hunger." Posted September 2007. U.S. Department of State, Volume 12, No. 9. www.america.gov/publications/ejournalusa/0907.html. Accessed August 9, 2010.
6. "Poverty Reduction and Equity." Posted 2010. The World Bank Group. Permanent URL for this page is http://go.worldbank.org/RQBDCTUXW0. Accessed August 9, 2010.
7. Roy Walmsley, "World Prison Population List (Eighth Edition)," International Centre for Prison Studies. January 26, 2009. King's College London—School of Law: http://www.kcl.ac.uk/depsta/law/research/icps/downloads/wppl-8th_41.pdf (accessed July 11, 2011).
8. "AIDS Epidemic Update." November, 2009. UNAIDS: 2009 Aids Epidemic Update. http://data.unaids.org/pub/Report/2009/JC1700_Epi_Update_2009_en.pdf. Accessed August 9, 2010.
9. British Social Attitudes Survey. *Future First*. December 2011 edition.
10. Office for National Statistics, *Religion in England and Wales 2011*, report dated 11 December 2012 (page 1).
11. Peter Brierley, *UK Church Statistics 2005-2015*.

Session 4: The Power of Vision

1. Bill Hybels, *Courageous Leadership* (Grand Rapids: Zondervan, 2002), 322.

Session 5: Vision — Overcoming Obstacles

1. Ken Boa, *Conformed to His Image* (Grand Rapids: Zondervan, 2001), 224–25.
2. Eugene H. Peterson, *Run with the Horses: The Quest for Life at Its Best*, 2nd ed. (Downers Grove, Ill.: InterVarsity Press, 2009), 41.
3. Leslie T. Lyall, *A Passion for the Impossible: The Continuing Story of the Mission Hudson Taylor Began* (London: OMF Books, 1965), 5.

Session 6: Culturally Relevant Evangelism

1. James D. Kennedy, *Evangelism Explosion* (Wheaton, IL: Tyndale House Publishers), 1970. Adapted with permission from the globally recognised Evangelism Explosion

International's training materials on personal testimony.

Session 8: Family Priority

1. Rick Warren, *The Purpose Driven Life: What on Earth Am I Here For?* (Grand Rapids: Zondervan, 2002), 117.
2. Defrain and Stinnett, *Strong Families around the World*, Family Matters 53 (winter 1999): 8–13. These six characteristics of strong families were reported by Nick Stinnett and John DeFrain in their book *Secrets of Strong Families* (Boston: Little, Brown & Co., 1986). They and their many colleagues have conducted further research in this area since then and have published several papers and articles about the amazing similarity of strong families from widely varying cultures.

Session 12: Living Christian to the Core

1. Eugene Peterson, *A Long Obedience in the Same Direction* (InterVarsity Press, 2000), 11.

Appendix

Additional Resources on Spiritual Gifts

There are many resources on spiritual gifts available online and in Christian bookstores. Suggested resources include:

Online Profile of the Nine Serving Gifts by Elmer Towns
> This profile focuses only on the nine serving, or task, gifts and can be found at www.ElmerTowns.com/spiritual_gifts_test.

Wagner, C. Peter, *Wagner modified Houts Spiritual Gifts Questionnaire.*
> This questionnaire is available for purchase. Individuals or small groups may choose to acquire the booklets and answer the questionnaire as part of this experience. Below, you will find an extensive and descriptive list of spiritual gifts based on the questionnaire. Each gift description includes supporting Biblical references.

Wagner, C. Peter, *Your Spiritual Gifts Can Help Your Church Grow* (Ventura, CA: Regal Books, 1979, 1994, 2005).
> This book is a companion to the Wagner-Houts Questionnaire and studies the gifts in detail.

Spiritual Gift Definitions
(Taken from www.BuildingChurch.net – Gifted2Serve,
Copyright ©2003 Building Church Ministries or Copyright ©2001 Andrew P Kulp)

1. Administration: "The ability to understand clearly the immediate and long-range goals of a particular unit of the body of Christ and to devise and execute effective plans for the accomplishment of those goals."

This gift is a leadership gift and is often characterised by people who lead the Body by steering others to remain on task. These people generally are concerned with the details of how to accomplish tasks, and tend to be masters at delegating specific tasks to other people according to their gifts and talents. Scriptures: Luke 14:28-30; Acts 6:1-7; 1 Corinthians 12:28; Titus 1:5.

2. Apostle: "The ability which enables them to assume and exercise helpful leadership over a number of churches in spiritual matters which is spontaneously recognised and appreciated by those churches." The Bible calls many others, beyond the Twelve and Paul, apostles: James (Gal 1:19), Barnabas (Acts 14:4, 14), Epaphroditus (Phil 2:25), Silas and Timothy (1 Thes 1:1, 2:6), Andronicas and Junia (Rom 16:7), and others (1 Cor 15:5, 7; 2 Cor 8:23; 11:13).

This gift is a leadership gift and is in continuing need today for the strengthening of churches and the establishment of new churches. This gift should be looked for in regional directors, church planters, and denominational leaders. Scriptures: 1 Corinthians 12:28; Ephesians 2:20; 4:11.

3. Deliverance: "The ability to cast out demons and evil spirits in the name of Jesus Christ."

This gift is a sign gift. Jesus gave his apostles the authority to cast out demons (Mark 3:14, 15; 6:13), and the gift was used during the earliest days of the church (Acts 15:16; 16:16-18). Those with this gift should be discerning in their use of it, and not develop an excessive preoccupation with demons and evil spirits. The Christian focus should be on the victory won in Jesus Christ and the salvation and abundant life he offers, not the ever-present forces of evil in this world. Scriptures: Matthew 12:22-32; Luke 10:12-20; Acts 8:5-8; 16:16-18; Romans 8:38-39; Ephesians 6:10-12.

4. Discerning of Spirits: "The ability to know with assurance whether certain behaviour purported to be of God is in reality divine, human, or Satanic."

This gift is a resourcing gift. Christians with this gift can recognise the true motives of people and also recognise when a person is distorting the truth or communicating error. This person often can recognise when Satan or other evil spirits are at work in a given person or situation. Scriptures: Matthew 16:21-23; Acts 5:1-11; 16:16-18; 17:11-16; 1 Corinthians 12:10; Hebrews 5:14; 1 John 4:1-6.

5. Evangelism: "The ability to readily share the Gospel with unbelievers in such a way that men and women often become Jesus' disciples and responsible members of the Body of Christ."

This gift is a communication gift. While the task of evangelism is an important spiritual exercise that all Christians should be involved with, God gifts certain members with an ability to have unusual sensitivity to when someone is ready to accept Christ, and will generally have greater success in leading people to Christ than other Christians. People with this gift should be active in training others to share their faith. Scriptures: Acts 8:5-6, 26-40; Ephesians 4:11-14; 2 Timothy 4:5.

6. Exhortation: "The ability to minister words of comfort, consolation, encouragement, and counsel to other members of the Body in such a way that they feel helped and healed."

This gift is a communication gift. This gift is often called "encouragement," but exhortation is used here because the gift is not limited to the connotations that the name "encouragement" implies. Those who use this gift within a teaching or ministry situation are often driven to give practical application to their insights. Often, those gifted in this area desire step-by-step plans of action to help others mature in Christ. Exhorters often find it natural to discover insights from personal experience when validated and amplified in Scripture. Scripture: Luke 3:16-18; Acts 11:23; 14:22; Romans 12:8; 1 Timothy 4:12; 5:1; Hebrews 10:25.

7. Faith: "The ability to discern with extraordinary confidence the will and purposes of God for his work."

This gift is a resourcing gift. All Christians are called to have faith, but some Christians seem to find it especially easy to trust God in difficult situations, or when he has given particularly spectacular promises. Those with this gift often scare other people with their confidence. People with this gift are often very irritated by criticism, as they consider it to be criticism against God and his will. Probably the biggest danger for those with this gift is that they often try to project their gift onto other people. Scriptures: Acts 11:22-24; 27:21-25; Romans 4:18-21; 1 Corinthians 12:9; Hebrews 11.

8. Giving: "The ability to contribute material resources to the work of the Lord with liberality and cheerfulness."

This gift is a practical gift. While all Christians should practice the discipline of giving through the minimum of 10% (tithe), God gifts certain members of the body to give remarkably greater amounts of their income with liberality and great joy. These people have an acute awareness that all they have belongs to the Lord and they are merely stewards. Therefore they know that God will supply their needs and richly bless them in their giving. Scriptures: Matthew 6:2-4; Mark 12:41-44; Romans 12:8; 1 Corinthians 13:3; 2 Corinthians 8:1-7; 9:2-8; Philippians 4:14-19.

9. Healing: "The ability to serve as human intermediaries through whom God cures illness and restores health apart from the use of natural means."

This gift is a sign gift. Many attribute the occurrence of supernatural healing to a certain level of faith. Those who have this gift must use it knowing that the healing only occurs within the limits of God's will, and therefore, miraculous healing will not always occur. Those with this gift must also recognise that God often chooses to use medical science to bring about healing in a person. Therefore, doctors and medicine are not obsolete. Scripture: Acts 3:1-10; 5:12-16; 9:32-35; 28:7-10; 1 Corinthians 12:9, 28.

10. Helps: "The ability to invest the talents a person has in the life and ministry of other members of the Body, thus enabling those others to increase the effectiveness of their own spiritual gifts."

This gift is a practical gift. People with this gift often enjoy doing routine tasks in order to free others to do the ministry God has called them to do. People with this gift are often not looking for recognition for the work they do. Scriptures: Mark 15:40-41; Luke 8:2-3; Acts 9:36; Romans 16:1-2; 1 Corinthians 12:28; 2 Timothy 1:16-18.

11. Hospitality: "The ability to provide an open house and a warm welcome to those in need of food and lodging."

This gift is a practical gift. Those with this gift have an acute awareness of visitors and have a desire to make all people feel welcome. People with this gift enjoy visitors in their home, and are usually not bothered if someone stops by and their home is not spotless. Those with this gift are a key to helping new people become a part of the group. Scriptures: Acts 16:14-15; Romans 12:9-13; 16:23; Hebrews 13:1-2; 1 Peter 4:9.

12. Intercession: "The ability to pray for extended periods of time on a regular basis and see frequent and specific answers to their prayers, to a degree much greater than that which is expected of the average Christian."

This gift is a resourcing gift. Those with this gift often feel compelled to pray for specific requests when they are made known. Gifted intercessors have a much greater occurrence of specific answers to prayer than most Christians. Intercessors often have an acute understanding that prayer is genuinely a conversation with God and, when left alone, find themselves engaged in prayer. Many intercessors experience times when God moves them to pray for situations when they are not entirely sure what they are praying for. To those who get to know intercessors well, prayer becomes contagious. Those with this gift should help others learn how to pray more effectively. Scriptures: Luke 22:41-44; Acts 12:12; Romans 8:26-27; Colossians 1:9-12; 4:12-13; 1 Timothy 2:1-2; James 5:14-16.

13. Interpretation of Tongues: "The ability to make known in the vernacular the message of one who speaks in tongues."

This gift is a sign gift. Those with this gift are used to bring the personal edification of tongues to a position where the message edifies the group in which the tongue was spoken. Those with this gift gain a sense of what God is trying to say when they hear a person speak in tongues. Should a person with this gift fail to interpret the tongue when it is spoken and they receive the interpretation through the Holy Spirit, they have done a great disservice to the person who spoke in tongues and to the group as the edification that God desires has not taken place. Often, the interpreter is also the person who has spoken in tongues. The interpretation of tongues is often closely related to the message given by an exhorter or a prophet. Scriptures: 1 Corinthians 12:10-30; 14:13-17, 26-28.

14. Knowledge: "The ability to discover, accumulate, analyse, and clarify information and ideas which are pertinent to the well-being of the Body."

This gift is a resourcing gift. Those with the gift of knowledge are at home in a book or studying. Those with this gift will often spend countless hours researching information. These people are interested in ideas and problem solving through gathering information and studying. Often, those with this gift have a low need for people. On rare occasions, people with this gift will gather vast amounts of information through studying and analysing personal experience, but the primary method of learning with this gift is reading and studying books and other written materials. Scriptures: Luke 1:1-4; Acts 5:1-11; 1 Corinthians 2:14; 12:8; 2 Corinthians 11:6; Colossians 1:10; 2:2-3; 1 Timothy 2:15.

15. Leadership: "The ability to set goals in accordance with God's purpose for the future and to communicate these goals to others in such a way that they voluntarily and harmoniously work together to accomplish those goals for the glory of God."

This gift is a leadership gift. People with this gift are often focused on the greater goal of the group and are not overly concerned with the details. Leaders delegate tasks and details to others to accomplish the greater goal. Leaders are visionaries. Leaders have followers. A visionary without followers is not a leader. Scriptures: Luke 9:51; Acts 6:1-7; 15:7-11; Romans 12:8; 1 Timothy 5:17; Hebrews 13:17.

16. Mercy: "The ability to feel genuine empathy and compassion for individuals (both Christian and non-Christian) who suffer from distressing physical, mental, or emotional problems, and to translate that compassion into cheerfully done deeds which reflect Christ's love and alleviate the suffering."

This gift is a practical gift. Those with this gift find themselves visiting and assisting those in need, and often feel the pain of the person they are helping within themselves. People with this gift find it extremely difficult not to help those who seem less fortunate than themselves. Those with this gift generally enjoy helping those with physical or mental problems and do well in ministries involving visiting hospitals, nursing homes, prisons, and those who are housebound. Scriptures: Matthew 20:29-34; 25:24-40; Mark 9:41; Luke 10:33-35; Acts 11:28-30; 16:33-34; Romans 12:8; Jude 22-23.

17. Miracles: "The ability to serve as human intermediaries through whom God performs powerful acts that are perceived by observers to have altered the ordinary course of nature."

This gift is a sign gift. This gift is manifested through the supernatural intervention by God into specific circumstances in order to change the perceived natural outcome. Those with this gift must recognise that God only causes miracles to happen in order to bring the greatest glory to himself. Scriptures: Acts 9:36-42; 19:11-20; 20:7-12; Romans 15:17-19; 1 Corinthians 1:22-25; 12:10, 28; 2 Corinthians 12:12.

18. Missionary: "The ability to minister whatever other spiritual gifts a person has in a culture other than their own."

This gift is a leadership gift. Those with this gift find it easy or exciting to adjust to a different culture or community. Missionaries find great joy working with minorities, people of other countries, or those with other distinct cultural differences. Those with this gift have a stronger-than-average desire to be a part of the fulfillment of the Great Commission around the world. Scriptures: Acts 8:4; 13:1-4; 22:21; Romans 10:15; 1 Corinthians 9:19-23.

19. Prophecy: "The ability to receive and communicate an immediate message of God to his people with authority and urgency perceived by the hearers."

This gift is a communication gift. Those with the gift of prophecy will often feel as though they have a direct word from God that will comfort, encourage, guide, warn, or rebuke the Body of Christ. Prophets are concerned about evangelism and will have a desire to speak strongly against evil in society or in the Church. Prophets have a great sense of urgency to their message. Unless paired with the gifts of exhortation or teaching, prophets will often not feel the need to explain their message, but will expect immediate response. The message of a prophet must always be tested in line with Scripture. Scripture: Luke 7:26; Acts 15:32; 21:9-11; Romans 12:6; 1 Corinthians 12:10, 28; 14:3, 24-25, 29, 36-38; Ephesians 4:11-14.

20. Service: "The ability to identify the unmet needs involved in a task related to God's work, and to make use of available resources to meet those needs and help accomplish the desired results."

This gift is a practical gift. Those with the gift of service enjoy doing routine tasks around the Church regardless of how they affect others. Those with this gift enjoy menial tasks and do them cheerfully. Service-oriented people would rather take orders than give them. Scripture: John 12:26; Acts 6:1-7; Romans 12:6-7; Galatians 6:2, 9-10; 2 Timothy 1:16-18; Titus 3:14.

21. Shepherd: "The ability to assume a long-term personal responsibility for the welfare of a group of believers."

This gift is a leadership gift. This gift is often called "pastor," however, that name has a connotations of a specific position in the Church. In actuality, when pastors have this gift, their ability to continue sustained growth in their churches is greatly diminished, as they tend to require a certain level of interaction with every member of their congregation. Those with the gift of shepherd have a great need for long-term relationships. Shepherds will sacrificially give themselves to other people in such a way that they are built-up in their faith. Shepherds take personal responsibility for the successes and failures of those in the group that they invest themselves in. Scriptures: John 10:1-18; Ephesians 4:11-14; 1 Timothy 3:1-7; 1 Peter 5:1-4.

22. Teaching: "The ability to communicate information relevant to the health and ministry of the Body and its members in such a way that others will learn."

This gift is a communication gift. People with the gift of teaching enjoy studying the Bible and related materials in order to communicate what they have learned to other Christians. Those with this gift find it easy to organise vast amounts of information in such a way as to make it easy to communicate, understand, and remember. Scriptures: Matthew 7:28-29; 28:19-20; Acts 15:32; Romans 12:6; 1 Corinthians 12:10, 28; Ephesians 4:11-14.

23. Tongues: "The ability (a) to speak to God in a language that they have never learned and/or (b) to receive and communicate a message of God to his people through a divinely anointed utterance in a language they never learned."

This gift is a sign gift. Tongues is often associated with intercession and/or faith, but must be recognised as not necessarily being the sign of the baptism of the Holy Spirit or even as evidence of the filling of the Holy Spirit. 1 Corinthians 13:1 suggests that there are two forms of the gift of tongues: tongues of men and tongues of angels. This would mean that the speaker could be speaking in an earthly language or in a language beyond normal human understanding. Scriptures: Mark 16:17; Acts 2:1-13; 10:44-46; 19:1-7; Romans 8:26-27; 1 Corinthians 12:10,28; 13:1; 14:13-19, 26-28, 39.

24. Voluntary Poverty: "The ability to renounce material comfort and luxury and adopt a personal lifestyle equivalent to those living at the poverty level in a given society in order to serve God more effectively."

This gift is a practical gift. Those with the spiritual gift of voluntary poverty will often choose to live among people who are considered poverty-stricken in a given area, and live at their level, although they have the means to live at a higher standard. The primary motivation for this choice is to minister more effectively to the people through identification. Scriptures: Acts 2:44-45; 4:34-27; 1 Corinthians 13:1-3; 2 Corinthians 8:9.

25. Wisdom: "The ability to know how given knowledge may best be applied to specific needs arising in the Body of Christ."

This gift is a resourcing gift. Those with this gift have an excellent ability to apply spiritual truth to everyday life. Often, people in the church naturally seek people with this gift when they are facing complicated spiritual problems. When a person with this gift considers past experience, they realise that they often make good and correct decisions and judgments. Scriptures: Proverbs 4:5-8; Acts 6:3, 10; 15:13-20; 20:20-21; Romans 12:17; 1 Corinthians 12:28; Ephesians 4:11-14; Colossians 1:28.

Notes

1) Many spiritual gifts inventories combine the gift of Apostle with the gift of Missionary because the Greek word is the same, meaning "sent one" – literally, one sent with authority or as an ambassador or representative. These gifts have been separated here with the distinction that the Missionary gift is focused on cross-cultural work, whereas the Apostle gift is focused on overseeing the expansion of the Church in a given area, regardless of culture.

2) Exhortation, Prophecy, and Teaching are all considered communication gifts. The distinctions for each gift are often confused. Often, gifted communicators have a mix of these gifts. Exhortation focuses on personal and practical application of the message or truth being communicated. Prophecy focuses purely on the message or truth to be communicated. Teaching focuses on bringing thorough or adequate understanding of the message or truth being communicated.

3) The gift of Giving is often associated with the gift of Voluntary Poverty, as many with the gift of Voluntary Poverty also have the gift of Giving. However, notice that the motivation for Voluntary Poverty is for effective ministry through identification with a group of less-fortunate people, whereas those with the gift if Giving are motivated by what their money can do towards God's work.

4) The gifts of Healing and Miracles are often combined, since they both involve the occurrence of events beyond natural means. However, one is focused on the healing of the human body, while the other is focused on other miraculous events that alter the ordinary course of nature. These may, in fact, be two separate manifestations of the same gift.

5) The gifts of Helps, Mercy, and Service are often confused. Helps focuses on Christian works and freeing others to accomplish their God-given ministries. Mercy focuses on people in distress and reflects God's love and compassion. Service focuses on accomplishing little tasks that may otherwise go undone in order to move the greater goal of the ministry or Church toward completion.